미국의 사회와 문화

American Society and Culture

| 이종문 著 |

JW 장원문화

책을 내면서

『미국의 사회와 문화』는 Wikipedia의 방대한 자료를 기반으로 미국의 사회와 문화를 쉽게 이해하고, 미국에 대한 다양한 정보를 영어 원문을 통해 접근하도록 도움을 주려는 의도에서 집필하게 되었습니다. 주지하다시피 Wikipedia는 2001년 1월 15일 Jimmy Wales가 만들고 비영리 단체인 Wikipedia 재단이 운영하는 온라인 백과사전으로서, 누구나 자유롭게 글을 쓸 수 있고 또 수정할 수 있는 특징을 갖고 있습니다. 따라서 이 책은 Wikipedia에서 미국의 사회와 문화와 관련된 흥미로운 주제들을 선정하여 그에 해당하는 영어 원문과 함께 간략한 내용을 설명하고 어려운 단어와 숙어를 정리하여 소개하고 있습니다. 무엇보다도 이 책은 미국의 초기 역사에서부터 현재에 이르기까지 미국의 정체성과 역사, 과학과 기술, 대학, 자동차, 스포츠, 자연, 이정표가 되는 장소, 식음료, 항공을 포함한 대중교통, 방송과 신문 및 시사 잡지를 포함한 언론, 하와이를 비롯한 대표적인 관광지와 도시 등 미국의 일상생활과 관련된 다양한 분야의 내용들을 다루고 있습니다. 이 책을 집필하면서 사용한 모든 자료는 Wikipedia의 해당 온라인 자료를 이용하고, Hawaii의 경우에는 Hawaii 관광청의 자료도 인용하며, 각각의 키워드에 각주를 달아 인용한 사이트의 주소를 밝혀두었습니다. 아무쪼록 이 책이 미국 사회와 문화에 관심을 갖고 영어를 공부하려는 학생들에게 작은 안내서가 되기를 바랍니다. 끝으로 오랫동안 필자의 책을 출판해주신 장원문화인쇄 출판의 원병철 사장님께 감사를 드립니다.

목 차

1. White House ·· 8
2. United States Capitol ··· 12
3. Statue of Liberty ··· 14
4. Central Park ·· 18
5. Empire State Building ··· 20
6. Carnegie Hall ·· 22
7. Wall Street ·· 24
8. Madison Square Garden ··· 26
9. World Trade Center ·· 28
10. Broadway ··· 30
11. Academy Awards ·· 32
12. Harlem ·· 34
13. Barnes & Noble ·· 36
14. Golden Gate Bridge ·· 38
15. Hollywood ··· 40
16. Disney Land ·· 42
17. Universal Studios ··· 44
18. Silicon Valley ·· 46
19. Grand Canyon ·· 48
20. Niagara Falls ·· 50

21. Yosemite National Park ·· 52

22. Death Valley ··· 54

23. Facebook ··· 56

24. twitter ··· 58

25. NASA ··· 60

26. FBI··· 62

27. CIA ·· 64

28. Harvard University ·· 66

29. Massachusetts Institute of Technology ······························· 68

30. Stanford University ··· 70

31. GM··· 72

32. Ford ··· 74

33. NBA ··· 76

34. CNN ··· 78

35. Voice of America ·· 80

36. AP ··· 82

37. Ted ·· 84

38. Time ··· 86

39. Newsweek ·· 88

40. The New York Times ··· 90

41. The Washington Post	92
42. Citibank	94
43. Black Friday	96
44. Halloween	98
45. Starbucks	100
46. McDonald's	102
47. KFC	104
48. Burger King	106
49. Popeyes	108
50. Subway	110
51. Taco Bell	112
52. Pizza Hut	114
53. Domino's Pizza	116
54. Coca-Cola	118
55. Pepsi Cola	120
56. Baskinrobbins	122
57. Amazon	124
58. Walmart	126
59. Sam's Club	128
60. Costco	130
61. FedEx	132

62. U-Haul ·· 134

63. Greyhound ··· 136

64. Amtrek ·· 138

65. American Airlines ··· 140

66. United Airlines ·· 142

67. Delta Airlines ·· 144

68. Washington D.C. ·· 146

69. New York ·· 148

70. Boston ·· 150

71. Los Angeles ·· 154

72. Las Vegas ··· 156

73. Alaska ·· 158

74. Hawaii ·· 160

75. Guam ·· 170

76. Saipan ·· 172

1. White House[*]

The White House is the official residence and workplace of the president of the United States. It is located at 1600 Pennsylvania Avenue NW in Washington, D.C. and has been the residence of every U.S. president since John Adams in 1800. The term is often used as a metonym for the president and his advisers.

The residence was designed by Irish-born architect James Hoban in the neoclassical style. Hoban modelled the building on Leinster House in Dublin, a building which today houses the Oireachtas, the Irish legislature. Construction took place between 1792 and 1800 using Aquia Creek sandstone painted white. When Thomas Jefferson moved into the house in 1801, he (with architect Benjamin Henry Latrobe) added low colonnades on each wing that concealed stables and storage. In 1814, during the War of 1812, the mansion was set ablaze by the British Army in the Burning of Washington, destroying the interior and charring much of the exterior. Reconstruction began almost immediately, and President James Monroe moved into the partially reconstructed Executive Residence in October 1817. Exterior construction continued with the addition of the semi-circular South portico in 1824 and the North portico in 1829.

---

[*] https://en.wikipedia.org/wiki/White_House

White House는 1800년 제2대 대통령 John Adams 이래로 모든 미국 대통령의 관저로 사용되어왔으며, "White House"라는 용어는 대통령과 그의 보좌관들을 위한 은유로 종종 사용된다. 아일랜드 태생의 건축가인 James Hoban이 신고전주의적인 스타일로 설계했고 하얗게 칠한 Aquia Creek 사암(砂岩)을 사용하여 1792년에서 1800년 사이에 건축되었다. 1814년 영국과의 전쟁 때 영국군에 의해 건물 내부가 파괴되고 바깥 대부분이 불에 타서 시꺼멓게 됐으나, 1817년 10월 곧바로 재건을 시작하고 바깥벽을 하얗게 칠한 것에서 이 명칭이 유래되었다.

Smart Vocabulary

official residence : 공관, 관저
metonym : 환유어(換喩語)
neoclassical : 신고전주의(파)의
legislature : 입법부, 입법 기관
sandstone : 〖지질〗 사암(砂岩)
colonnade : 열주(列柱), 주랑
stable: 마구간; 가축우리
ablaze : (활활) 타오르고, 화염에 싸여서
char : 숯으로 만들다; (시꺼멓게) 태우다
portico : 주랑(柱廊) 현관

Because of crowding within the executive mansion itself, President Theodore Roosevelt had all work offices relocated to the newly constructed West Wing in 1901. Eight years later in 1909, President William Howard Taft expanded the West Wing and created the first Oval Office, which was eventually moved as the section was expanded. In the main mansion, the third-floor attic was converted to living quarters in 1927 by augmenting the existing hip roof with long shed dormers. A newly constructed East Wing was used as a reception area for social events; Jefferson's colonnades connected the new wings. East Wing alterations were completed in 1946, creating additional office space. By 1948, the residence's load-bearing exterior walls and internal wood beams were found to be close to failure. Under Harry S. Truman, the interior rooms were completely dismantled and a new internal load-bearing steel frame constructed inside the walls. Once this work was completed, the interior rooms were rebuilt.

The modern-day White House complex includes the Executive Residence, West Wing, East Wing, the Eisenhower Executive Office Building — the former State Department, which now houses offices for the president's staff and the vice president — and Blair House, a guest residence. The Executive Residence is made up of six stories — the Ground Floor, State Floor, Second Floor, and Third Floor, as well as a two-story basement. The property is a National Heritage Site owned by the National Park Service and is part of the President's Park. In 2007, it was ranked second on the American Institute of Architects list of "America's Favorite Architecture".

Smart Vocabulary

Oval Office: 대통령 집무실
attic: 고미다락(방)
convert: 전환하다, 바꾸다
augment: 늘리다, 증대시키다
hip: 〖건축〗 추녀마루, 귀마루
shed: (빛·열·향기 등을) 발(산)하다
dormer: 〖건축〗 지붕창, 천창
alteration: 변경; 개조
dismantle: (건물·배에서) 설비를(기구·장비·방비 등을) 제거하다

2. United States Capitol[*]

The White House is the official residence and workplace of the president of the United States. It is located at 1600 Pennsylvania Avenue NW in Washington, D.C. and has been the residence of every U.S. president since John Adams in 1800. The term is often used as a metonym for the president and his advisers.

The residence was designed by Irish-born architect James Hoban in the neoclassical style. Hoban modelled the building on Leinster House in Dublin, a building which today houses the Oireachtas, the Irish legislature. Construction took place between 1792 and 1800 using Aquia Creek sandstone painted white. When Thomas Jefferson moved into the house in 1801, he (with architect Benjamin Henry Latrobe) added low colonnades on each wing that concealed stables and storage. In 1814, during the War of 1812, the mansion was set ablaze by the British Army in the Burning of Washington, destroying the interior and charring much of the exterior. Reconstruction began almost immediately, and President James Monroe moved into the partially reconstructed Executive Residence in October 1817. Exterior construction continued with the addition of the semi-circular South portico in 1824 and the North portico in 1829.

---

[*] https://en.wikipedia.org/wiki/United_States_Capitol

United States Capitol은 Washington D.C.에 있는 National Mall의 동쪽 끝에 있는 Capitol Hill에 위치한 국회의사당 건물이다. 원래 이 건물은 1800년에 완성되었으나, 1814년 Washington이 불타면서 Capitol이 일시적으로 사용할 수 없게 되었다. 건물이 5년 만에 완전히 복구되었고, 이후 증축되어 거대한 돔이 추가되고, 양원제 의회를 위해 남쪽 건물에 하원, 북쪽 건물에 상원이 확장되었다. 행정부와 사법부의 주요 건물들처럼, 국회 의사당은 독특한 신고전주의 스타일로 지어졌고 흰색 외관을 갖고 있다.

Smart Vocabulary

Congress: 의회, 국회
legislative: 입법(상)의; 입법부의
Federal District: 연방구
quadrant: 사분면(四分面)
render: …로 만들다, …이 되게 하다
consequence: 결과
the bicameral legislature: 양원제 의회(Lower(Upper) Chamber 하원(상원))
the House of Representatives: 하원
Senate: 상원
executive: 행정(상)의; 행정부에 속하는
judicial: 사법의
dignitary: (정부의) 고관

3. Statue of Liberty *

The Statue of Liberty (Liberty Enlightening the World) is a colossal neoclassical sculpture on Liberty Island in New York Harbor in New York, in the United States. The copper statue, a gift from the people of France to the people of the United States, was designed by French sculptor Frédéric Auguste Bartholdi and its metal framework was built by Gustave Eiffel. The statue was dedicated on October 28, 1886.

The Statue of Liberty is a figure of Libertas, a robed Roman liberty goddess. She holds a torch above her head with her right hand, and in her left hand carries a *tabula ansata* inscribed in Roman numerals with "JULY IV MDCCLXXVI" (July 4, 1776), the date of the U.S. Declaration of Independence. A broken shackle and chain lie at her feet as she walks forward, commemorating the recent national abolition of slavery. The statue became an icon of freedom and of the United States, and a national park tourism destination. It is a welcoming sight to immigrants arriving from abroad.

---

* https://en.wikipedia.org/wiki/Statue_of_Liberty

The Statue of Liberty("세계를 비추는 자유")는 New York Harbor의 Liberty Island에 세워진 거대한 신고전주의적인 조각상으로, 프랑스가 1886년에 미국 독립 100주년을 기념하여 선물한 것이다. 이 조각상은 프랑스 조각가 Frédéric Auguste Bartholdi가 자신의 어머니를 모델로 만들고, 금속 뼈대는 Eiffel Tower를 설계한 Gustave Eiffel이 만들었다고 알려져 있다. 이 조각상은 1886년 10월 28일에 헌납되었다. The Statue of Liberty는 로마의 자유의 여신인 Libertas의 모습으로서, 오른손으로는 머리 위로 횃불을 들고 왼손에는 로마 숫자로 1776년 7월 4일이라는 날짜가 새겨진 독립 선언서를 들고 있다. 그녀가 앞으로 걸을 때 발 앞에 부러진 걸쇠와 사슬이 놓여 있는 것은 노예제 폐지를 기념하는 것이다. The Statue of Liberty는 American Dream을 안고 New York Harbor로 들어오는 이민자들에게 자유와 미국의 상징이 되었다.

Smart Vocabulary

sculpture: 조각(술), 조각 작품
inscribe: 새기다
shackle: 쇠고랑, 수갑, 족쇄, 차꼬(fetters)
commemorate: (…을) 기념하다, 축하하다
abolition: 폐지

Bartholdi was inspired by a French law professor and politician, Édouard René de Laboulaye, who is said to have commented in 1865 that any monument raised to U.S. independence would properly be a joint project of the French and U.S. peoples. Because of the post-war instability in France, work on the statue did not commence until the early 1870s. In 1875, Laboulaye proposed that the French finance the statue and the U.S. provide the site and build the pedestal. Bartholdi completed the head and the torch-bearing arm before the statue was fully designed, and these pieces were exhibited for publicity at international expositions.

The torch-bearing arm was displayed at the Centennial Exposition in Philadelphia in 1876, and in Madison Square Park in Manhattan from 1876 to 1882. Fundraising proved difficult, especially for the Americans, and by 1885 work on the pedestal was threatened by lack of funds. Publisher Joseph Pulitzer, of the New York World, started a drive for donations to finish the project and attracted more than 120,000 contributors, most of whom gave less than a dollar. The statue was built in France, shipped overseas in crates, and assembled on the completed pedestal on what was then called Bedloe's Island. The statue's completion was marked by New York's first ticker-tape parade and a dedication ceremony presided over by President Grover Cleveland.

Smart Vocabulary

instability: 불안정
commence: 시작하다
pedestal: 주춧대, 기초
crate: 상자
ticker-tape: (환영을 위해 빌딩 창문 등에서 던지는) 색종이 테이프
dedication: 《美》 개관(식), 개통(식), 제막(식)
preside: 사회하다

4. Central Park *

Central Park is an urban park in Manhattan, New York City, located between the Upper West Side and the Upper East Side. Central Park is the most visited urban park in the United States, with an estimated 37.5–38 million visitors annually, and one of the most filmed locations in the world. Central Park is the fifth-largest park in New York City by area, covering 843 acres (3.41 km2).

Central Park was first approved in 1853 as a 778-acre (3.15 km2) park. In 1857, landscape architect Frederick Law Olmsted and architect/landscape designer Calvert Vaux won a design competition to construct the park with a plan they titled the "Greensward Plan". Construction began the same year, and the park's first areas were opened to the public in late 1858. Additional land at the northern end of Central Park was purchased in 1859, and the park was completed in 1876. After a period of decline in the early 20th century, New York City parks commissioner Robert Moses started a program to clean up Central Park. Another decline in the late 20th century spurred the creation of the Central Park Conservancy in 1980, which refurbished many parts of the park during the 1980s and 1990s.

Main attractions of the park include landscapes such as the Ramble and Lake, Hallett Nature Sanctuary, the Jacqueline Kennedy Onassis Reservoir, and Sheep Meadow; amusement attractions such as Wollman Rink, Central Park Carousel, and the Central Park Zoo; formal spaces such as the Central Park Mall and Bethesda Terrace; and the Delacorte Theater, which hosts Shakespeare in the Park programs in the summertime. The park also has sports facilities, including the North Meadow Recreation Center, basketball courts, baseball fields, and soccer fields.

---

* https://en.wikipedia.org/wiki/Central_Park

Central Park는 New York City의 Manhattan의 Upper West Side와 the Upper East Side 사이에 위치한 도시공원이다. 이 공원은 1853년에 승인받은 후 Frederick Law Olmsted 와 Calvert Vaux가 "Greensward Plan"라는 제목으로 공원을 건축하기로 계획하여 디자인 대회에서 우승했다. 이 공원은 Ramble and Lake, Hallett Nature Sanctuary, the Jacqueline Kennedy Onassis Reservoir, and Sheep Meadow, Wollman Rink, Central Park Carousel, and the Central Park Zoo Central Park Mall and Bethesda Terrace; and the Delacorte Theater 등의 시설과 North Meadow Recreation Center와 같은 스포츠 시설을 갖고 있으며, 1963년 National Historic Landmark로 지정된다.

Smart Vocabulary

estimate: 어림잡다, 견적하다, 산정하다
approve: 승인하다, 허가[인가]하다
landscape architect: 조경 설계사, 정원 설계사; 풍치 도시 계획 기사
greensward: 잔디
commissioner: (정부가 임명한) 위원, 이사; 국장, 지방 행정관
spur: …에 박차를 가하다
conservancy: (자연 등의) 보존, 보호, 관리
refurbish: 다시 닦다[윤내다], 다시 갈다; …을 일신[쇄신]하다
ramble: 소요, 산책
sanctuary: 성역, 보호 구역
reservoir: 저장소; 저수지
carousel: 회전목마

5. Empire State Building [*]

The Empire State Building is a 102-story[c] Art Deco skyscraper in Midtown Manhattan, New York City. It was designed by Shreve, Lamb & Harmon and completed in 1931. The building has a roof height of 1,250 feet (380 m) and stands a total of 1,454 feet (443.2 m) tall, including its antenna. Its name is derived from "Empire State", the nickname of New York, which is of unknown origin. The Empire State Building stood as the world's tallest building for nearly 40 years until the completion of the World Trade Center's North Tower in Lower Manhattan in late-1970. Following the September 11 attacks in 2001, it was again the tallest building in New York City until the new One World Trade Center surpassed it while under construction in April 2012. As of 2019, the building is the seventh-tallest building in New York City, the sixth-tallest completed skyscraper in the United States, and the 45th-tallest in the world. It is also the sixth-tallest freestanding structure in the Americas.

The site of the Empire State Building, located in Midtown South on the west side of Fifth Avenue between West 33rd and 34th Streets, was originally part of an early 18th-century farm, then became the site of the Waldorf–Astoria Hotel in 1893. In 1929, Empire State Inc. acquired the site and devised plans for a skyscraper there. The design for the Empire State Building was changed fifteen times until it was ensured to be the world's tallest building. Construction started on March 17, 1930, and the building opened thirteen and a half months afterward on May 1, 1931. Despite the publicity surrounding the building's construction, its owners failed to make a profit until the early 1950s. However, since its opening, the building's Art Deco architecture and open-air observation deck has made it a popular attraction, with around 4 million tourists from around the world visiting the building's 86th and 102nd floor observatories every year.

---

[*] https://en.wikipedia.org/wiki/Empire_State_Building

Empire State Building은 New York City의 Manhattan에 있는 지상 102층 높이의 아르 데코 마천루로서, "Empire State"이라는 이름은 New York의 별명에서 유래를 찾을 수 있다. World Trade Center가 완공되기 전에는 거의 40년 동안 세계에서 가장 높은 건물이었으나, 2001년 9.11 테러 이후 다시 New York City에서 가장 높은 건물이 된다.

Smart Vocabulary

art deco: 《F.》 아르 데코(1920-30년대의 장식적인 디자인으로, 1960년대에 부활)
skyscraper: 마천루, 고층건물
derive: 끌어내다, …의 기원을(유래를) 찾다
freestanding: 그 자체의 독립 구조로 서 있는
ensure: …을 책임지다, 보장(보증)하다, (성공 등을) 확실하게 하다
publicity: 명성, 평판; 공표, 공개
observation: 관찰, 관측
observatory: 전망대

6. Carnegie Hall *

Carnegie Hall is a concert venue in Midtown Manhattan in New York City, United States, located at 881 Seventh Avenue, occupying the east side of Seventh Avenue between West 56th Street and West 57th Street, two blocks south of Central Park.

Designed by architect and built by philanthropist in 1891, it is one of the most prestigious venues in the world for both classical music and popular music. Carnegie Hall has its own artistic programming, development, and marketing departments, and presents about 250 performances each season. It is also rented out to performing groups. The hall has not had a resident company since 1962, when the New York Philharmonic moved to Lincoln Center's Philharmonic Hall (renamed Avery Fisher Hall in 1973 and David Geffen Hall in 2015).

Carnegie Hall has 3,671 seats, divided among its three auditoriums.

---

* https://en.wikipedia.org/wiki/Carnegie_Hall

Carnegie Hall은 New York City의 Midtown Manhattan에 있는 콘서트홀로서 건축가William Burnet Tuthill이 설계하고 자선사업가 Andrew Carnegie가 1891년에 건축했으며 매 시즌 약 250개의 공연을 한다.

Smart Vocabulary

venue: (경기·회의 등의) 개최(지정)지
philanthropist: 박애가(주의자), 자선가
prestigious: 명성 있는; 유명한
auditorium: 청중(관객)석, 방청석; 강당, 큰 강의실; 회관

7. Wall Street [*]

Wall Street is an eight-block-long street running roughly northwest to southeast from Broadway to South Street, at the East River, in the Financial District of Lower Manhattan in New York City. Over time, the term has become a metonym for the financial markets of the United States as a whole, the American financial services industry (even if financial firms are not physically located there), or New York–based financial interests.

Anchored by Wall Street, New York City has been called both the most economically powerful city and the leading financial center of the world, and the city is home to the world's two largest stock exchanges by total market capitalization, the New York Stock Exchange and NASDAQ. Several other major exchanges have or had headquarters in the Wall Street area, including the New York Mercantile Exchange, the New York Board of Trade, and the former American Stock Exchange.

---

[*] https://en.wikipedia.org/wiki/Wall_Street

Wall Street는 New York City의 Lower Manhattan 금융지역에서 여덟 블록의 거리지만, 시간이 지나면서 이 용어는 미국의 금융 시장, 미국의 금융 서비스 산업(금융 회사가 실제로 그 곳에 있지 않더라도) 또는 New York에 기반을 둔 금융 이해관계를 상징하게 되었다. Wall Street는 세계 최고의 금융 중심지로서 New York Stock Exchange과 NASDAQ과 같이 총 시가 총액으로 세계에서 가장 큰 두 개의 주식 거래소의 본거지이다.

Smart Vocabulary

term: 말;《특히》술어, 용어
metonym: 〚修〛환유어(換喩語)
physically: 실제로, 눈에 보이는 형태로서
interest: (종종 pl.) 이익; 이해관계
stock exchange: (종종 S- E-) 증권 거래소
capitalization: 자본화; 현금화; (수입・재산의) 자본 평가, 주식 자본
mercantile: 상인의, 장사(상업)의

8. Madison Square Garden *

Madison Square Garden, colloquially known as The Garden or in initials as MSG, is a multi-purpose indoor arena in New York City. Located in Midtown Manhattan between 7th and 8th Avenues from 31st to 33rd Streets, it is situated atop Pennsylvania Station. It is the fourth venue to bear the name "Madison Square Garden"; the first two (1879 and 1890) were located on Madison Square, on East 26th Street and Madison Avenue, with the third Madison Square Garden (1925) further uptown at Eighth Avenue and 50th Street.

The Garden is used for professional ice hockey and basketball, as well as boxing, concerts, ice shows, circuses, professional wrestling and other forms of sports and entertainment. It is close to other midtown Manhattan landmarks, including the Empire State Building, Koreatown, and Macy's at Herald Square. It is home to the New York Rangers of the National Hockey League (NHL), the New York Knicks of the National Basketball Association (NBA), and was home to the New York Liberty (WNBA) from 1997 to 2017.

Originally called Madison Square Garden Center, the Garden opened on February 11, 1968, and is the oldest major sporting facility in the New York metropolitan area.

---

* https://en.wikipedia.org/wiki/Madison_Square_Garden

"The Garden" 또는 MSG"로 알려진 Madison Square Garden은 New York City의 다목적 실내 경기장으로서 Pennsylvania Station 위에 위치하고 있으며, 같은 이름을 가진 네 번째 장소라고 하여 Madison Square Garden4라고도 한다. NHL의 New York Rangers의 홈구장이고, NBA의 New York Knicks의 홈구장이며, WNBA의 New York Liberty의 홈구장이다.

Smart Vocabulary

colloquially: 구어로, 회화체로
arena: 경기장
atop: …의 정상에

9. World Trade Center *

The original World Trade Center was a large complex of seven buildings in the Financial District of Lower Manhattan, New York City, United States. It opened on April 4, 1973, and was destroyed in 2001 during the September 11 attacks. At the time of their completion, the Twin Towers — the original 1 World Trade Center, at 1,368 feet (417 m); and 2 World Trade Center, at 1,362 feet (415.1 m) — were the tallest buildings in the world. Other buildings in the complex included the Marriott World Trade Center (3 WTC), 4 WTC, 5 WTC, 6 WTC, and 7 WTC. The complex contained 13,400,000 square feet (1,240,000 m²) of office space.

On the morning of September 11, 2001, Al-Qaeda-affiliated hijackers flew two Boeing 767 jets into the North and South Towers within minutes of each other; two hours later, both towers collapsed. The attacks killed 2,606 people in and within the vicinity of the towers, as well as all 157 on board the two aircraft. Falling debris from the towers, combined with fires that the debris initiated in several surrounding buildings, led to the partial or complete collapse of all the buildings in the complex, and caused catastrophic damage to ten other large structures in the surrounding area.

The cleanup and recovery process at the World Trade Center site took eight months, during which the remains of the other buildings were demolished. A new World Trade Center complex is being built with six new skyscrapers and several other buildings, many of which have already been completed. A memorial and museum to those killed in the attacks, a new rapid transit hub, and an elevated park have been opened. One World Trade Center, the tallest building in the Western Hemisphere at 1,776 feet (541 m), is the lead building for the new complex, and was completed in November 2014.

---

* https://en.wikipedia.org/wiki/Madison_Square_Garden

World Trade Center는 New York City의 Manhattan 금융가에 위치한 7개 건물로 이루어진 복합 건물로서, 1973년 4월 4일에 개장했으나 9.11 테러로 인해 2001년에 붕괴되었다. 완공 당시 세계에서 가장 높은 빌딩이었으나, 1975년 2월 13일 화재, 1993년 2월 26일 폭탄 테러를 당했으며, 1998년 1월 14일 강도 사건 등의 사고가 있었고, 1998년 New York과 New Jersey 항만위원회가 민영화를 결정했다. 2001년 9월 11일 붕괴 이후 World Trade Center의 잔해를 청소하고 복구하는데 8개월이 걸렸으며, 이후 이 잔해위에 건설된 One World Trade Center는 2014년 11월에 완공되었다.

Smart Vocabulary

affiliate: 가입시키다, 회원으로 하다; 관계를 맺다
vicinity: 가까움, 근접; 가까운 곳, 부근
debris: 부스러기, 파편(의 더미)
initiate: 시작하다
partial: 부분적인, 일부분의
catastrophe: 대이변; 큰 재해
remains: (보통 pl.) 잔존물, 유해
demolish: (건물 따위를) 부수다
transit: 통과, 통행; 횡단; 운송
elevate: (들어) 올리다, 높이다

10. Broadway *

Broadway is a road in the U.S. state of New York. Broadway runs from State Street at Bowling Green for 13 mi (21 km) through the borough of Manhattan and 2 mi (3.2 km) through the Bronx, exiting north from the city to run an additional 18 mi (29 km) through the municipalities of Yonkers, Hastings-On-Hudson, Dobbs Ferry, Irvington, and Tarrytown, and terminating north of Sleepy Hollow in Westchester County.

It is the oldest north–south main thoroughfare in New York City, with much of the current street beginning as the Wickquasgeck trail before the arrival of Europeans. This formed the basis for one of the primary thoroughfares of the Dutch New Amsterdam colony, which continued under British rule, although most of it did not bear its current name until the late 19th century.

Broadway in Manhattan is known widely as the heart of the American commercial theatrical industry, and is used as a metonym for it, as well as in the names of alternative theatrical ventures such as Off-Broadway and Off-Off-Broadway.

---

* https://en.wikipedia.org/wiki/Broadway_(Manhattan)

Broadway는 Manhattan의 중심지인 Times Square 주변에 있는 극장가이며, 이 도로는 New York City에서 가장 오래된 남북 주요 도로이다. Broadway는 미국 상업 연극 산업의 중심지로서 널리 알려져 있으며, 미국의 연극이나 뮤지컬계를 일컫는 말로 쓰이기도 한다.

Smart Vocabulary

borough: 《美》 자치 읍면 《어떤 주의》; (New York시의) 독립구
municipality: 자치체《시 · 읍 등》; 시(읍)당국
terminate: 끝내다; 경계를 짓다
thoroughfare: 통로, 가로; 주요 도로
metonym: [修] 환유어(換喩語)
alternative: 대체되는, 대신의; 달리 택할

11. Academy Awards [*]

The Academy Awards, more popularly known as the Oscars, are awards for artistic and technical merit in the film industry. Given annually by the Academy of Motion Picture Arts and Sciences (AMPAS), the awards are an international recognition of excellence in cinematic achievements as assessed by the Academy's voting membership. The various category winners are awarded a copy of a golden statuette, officially called the "Academy Award of Merit", although more commonly referred to by its nickname, the "Oscar". The statuette depicts a knight rendered in the Art Deco style.

The award was originally sculpted by George Stanley from a design sketch by Cedric Gibbons. AMPAS first presented it in 1929 at a private dinner hosted by Douglas Fairbanks in the Hollywood Roosevelt Hotel in what would become known as the 1st Academy Awards. The Academy Awards ceremony was first broadcast by radio in 1930 and was televised for the first time in 1953. It is the oldest worldwide entertainment awards ceremony and is now televised live worldwide. It is also the oldest of the four major annual American entertainment awards; its other three equivalents – the Emmy Awards for television, the Tony Awards for theater, and the Grammy Awards for music – are modeled after the Academy Awards.

---

[*] https://en.wikipedia.org/wiki/Academy_Awards

The Academy Awards는 Oscars로 더 잘 알려져 있으며, Academy의 투표로 평가되는 영화적 성과의 우수성을 국제적으로 인정하는 상으로서 Academy of Motion Picture Arts and Sciences(AMPAS)가 매년 수여한다. 다양한 부문의 수상자들은 공식적으로 "Academy Award of Merit""라고 불리는 황금 조각상을 받게 되는데, 그 조각상은 Art Deco 양식으로 그려진 기사(knight)를 묘사하고 있다.

Smart Vocabulary

assess: 평가하다
statuette: 작은 조상(彫像)
depict: 그리다; 묘사(서술, 표현)하다
Art Deco: 1920~30년대에 유행한 장식 미술의 한 양식. 기하학적 무늬와 강렬한 색채가 특징
render: …로 만들다; 표현하다, 묘사하다
equivalent: 동등한 것, 등가(등량)물; 상당하는 것
inception: 처음, 시작, 개시, 발단
sculpt: 조각(술)(=sculpture)

12. Harlem [*]

Harlem is a neighborhood in the northern section of the New York City borough of Manhattan. It is bounded roughly by Frederick Douglass Boulevard, St. Nicholas Avenue, and Morningside Park on the west; the Harlem River and 155th Street on the north; Fifth Avenue on the east; and Central Park North on the south. The greater Harlem area encompasses several other neighborhoods and extends west to the Hudson River, north to 155th Street, east to the East River, and south to 96th Street.

Originally a Dutch village, formally organized in 1658, it is named after the city of Haarlem in the Netherlands. Harlem's history has been defined by a series of economic boom-and-bust cycles, with significant population shifts accompanying each cycle. Harlem was predominantly occupied by Jewish and Italian Americans in the 19th century, but African-American residents began to arrive in large numbers during the Great Migration in the 20th century. In the 1920s and 1930s, Central and West Harlem were the focus of the "Harlem Renaissance", a major African-American cultural movement. With job losses during the Great Depression of the 1930s and the deindustrialization of New York City after World War II, rates of crime and poverty increased significantly. In the 21st century, crime rates decreased significantly, and Harlem started to gentrify.

---

[*] https://en.wikipedia.org/wiki/Harlem

Harlem은 원래 1658년 공식적으로 조직된 Netherlands 마을로서, Netherlands의 Haarlem 시의 이름을 따서 지은 것이다. Harlem의 역사는 일련의 경제적인 호황과 불황이 교체하는 것으로 정의되어 왔으며, 그것이 교체되는 것에 따라 상당한 인구 변화가 수반됐다. 19세기에 Harlem은 주로 유대계와 이탈리아계 미국인들이 거주했으나, 20세기 흑인 대이동 기간 동안 아프리카계 미국인 거주자들이 대거 이주했다. 1920년대와 1930년대에 Harlem의 중앙과 서쪽 지역은 아프리카계 미국인의 문화 운동인 "Harlem Renaissance"의 중심지였다. 1930년대 대공황 시기의 일자리 감소와 2차 세계 대전 이후 New York City의 제조업의 쇠퇴로 인해 범죄율과 빈곤율이 상당히 증가했다. 21세기에 범죄율은 상당히 감소했고, Harlem은 고급 주택지화 되기 시작했다.

Smart Vocabulary

bound: …의 경계가 되다; [수동태] (…와) 경계를 접하다《on; in; by》
encompass: 둘러(에워)싸다
boom-and-bust: 벼락 경기와 불경기의 교체
predominantly: 대개, 대부분
occupy: …에 거주하다, 점유하다
Great Migration: 흑인 대이동
Great Depression: 세계 대공황《1929년 미국에서 시작된》
deindustrialization: 제조업의 쇠퇴, 산업의 공동화
gentrify: 고급 주택(지)화하다; 고급화하다.

13. Barnes & Noble *

Barnes & Noble, Inc., is an American bookseller. It is a Fortune 1000 company and the bookseller with the largest number of retail outlets in the United States. As of March 7, 2019, the company operates 627 retail stores in all 50 U.S. states. In August 2019, Elliott Management Corporation acquired the company.

Barnes & Noble operates mainly through its Barnes & Noble Booksellers chain of bookstores. The company's headquarters are at 122 Fifth Avenue in New York City.

After a series of mergers and bankruptcies in the American bookstore industry since the 1990s, Barnes & Noble stands alone as the United States' largest national bookstore chain. Previously, Barnes & Noble operated the chain of small B. Dalton Bookseller stores in malls until they announced the liquidation of the chain. The company was also one of the nation's largest manager of college textbook stores located on or near many college campuses when that division was spun off as a separate public company called Barnes & Noble Education in 2015.

The company is known by its customers for large retail outlets, many of which contain a café serving Starbucks coffee and other consumables. Most stores sell books, magazines, newspapers, DVDs, graphic novels, gifts, games, toys, music, and Nook e-readers and tablets.

---

* https://en.wikipedia.org/wiki/Barnes_%26_Noble

Barnes & Noble은 1886년 New York City의 Cooper Union Building에 위치한 Arthur Hinds & Company 서점으로 시작했다. 1886년 가을, Massachusetts 주 Westfield 출신의 Harvard 졸업생인 Gilbert Clifford Noble이 그곳에 점원으로 고용되었고, 1894년에 파트너가 되었으며 서점의 이름을 Hinds & Noble로 바꾼다. Barnes & Noble은 Fortune 1000대 기업이며 2019년 3월 7일 현재 미국 50개의 주에 627개의 매장을 운영하고 있다.

Smart Vocabulary

acquire: 손에 넣다, 획득하다; (재산 · 권리 등을)
merger: 합병
liquidation: 청산, 상환
spin off: (회사 · 자산 등을) 분리 신설하다
public company: 주식회사
consumables: (보통 pl.) 소모품
graphic novel: 만화 소설

14. Golden Gate Bridge *

The Golden Gate Bridge is a suspension bridge spanning the Golden Gate, the one-mile-wide (1.6 km) strait connecting San Francisco Bay and the Pacific Ocean. The structure links the American city of San Francisco, California—the northern tip of the San Francisco Peninsula—to Marin County, carrying both U.S. Route 101 and California State Route 1 across the strait. The bridge is one of the most internationally recognized symbols of San Francisco, California, and the United States. It has been declared one of the Wonders of the Modern World by the American Society of Civil Engineers.

The Frommer's travel guide describes the Golden Gate Bridge as "possibly the most beautiful, certainly the most photographed, bridge in the world." At the time of its opening in 1937, it was both the longest and the tallest suspension bridge in the world, with a main span of 4,200 feet (1,280 m) and a total height of 746 feet (227 m).

---

* https://en.wikipedia.org/wiki/Golden_Gate_Bridge

Golden Gate Bridge는 California주 Golden Gate 해협에 위치한 현수교로서 San Francisco와 Marin County를 연결한다. 이 다리는 Joseph Strauss가 설계하고, 1933년에 착공하여 1937년에 준공하였으며 이후 San Francisco와 미국을 대표하는 상징이 된다. 이 다리의 건설은 1996년 미국토목학회(ASCE) 선정 현대 7대 불가사의 중 하나이다.

Smart Vocabulary

suspension bridge: 현수교
span: (강·계곡 따위에) 걸치다, 걸리다
strait: 해협

15. Hollywood *

Hollywood is a neighborhood in the central region of Los Angeles, California, notable as the home of the U.S. film industry, including several of its historic studios. Its name has come to be a shorthand reference for the industry and the people associated with it.

Hollywood was incorporated as a municipality in 1903. It was consolidated with the city of Los Angeles in 1910 and soon thereafter, a prominent film industry emerged, eventually becoming the most recognizable film industry in the world.

Development

In 1923, a large sign, reading HOLLYWOODLAND, was built in the Hollywood Hills. Its purpose was to advertise a housing development. In 1949, the Hollywood Chamber of Commerce entered a contract with the City of Los Angeles to repair and rebuild the sign. The agreement stipulated that "LAND" be removed to spell "HOLLYWOOD" so the sign would now refer to the district, rather than the housing development.

---

* https://en.wikipedia.org/wiki/Hollywood

Hollywood는 Los Angeles의 중심 지역에 위치하고 있으며, 몇몇 역사적인 스튜디오를 포함한 미국 영화 산업의 본거지로 유명하다. Hollywood라는 이름은 영화 산업과 그것과 관련된 사람들을 가리키는 말이 되었다. 1923년 Hollywood Hills에 세워진 큰 간판의 목적은 주택 개발을 광고하는 것이었다. 1949년 Hollywood Chamber of Commerce는 City of Los Angeles와 이 간판을 수리하고 다시 세우는 계약을 했다. 이 협정은 "HOLLYWOODLAND"에서 "LAND"를 삭제하도록 규정했고, 이 간판은 이제 주택 개발이 아닌 그 지역을 가리키게 되었다.

Smart Vocabulary

shorthand: 약칭; 속기(의)
reference: 언급
associated: (관련)된
incorporate: 통합(합병, 편입)하다
municipality: 자치체(시·읍 등)
consolidate: 통합(합병)하다
prominent: 현저한, 두드러진; 저명한
stipulate: …을 규정하다, 명기(명문화)하다; 조건으로서 요구하다, 약정(계약)하다
refer: 언급하다

16. Disney Land *

Disneyland Park, originally Disneyland, is the first of two theme parks built at the Disneyland Resort in Anaheim, California, opened on July 17, 1955. It is the only theme park designed and built to completion under the direct supervision of Walt Disney. It was originally the only attraction on the property; its official name was changed to Disneyland Park to distinguish it from the expanding complex in the 1990s. It is the oldest Disney Park in the world.

Walt Disney came up with the concept of Disneyland after visiting various amusement parks with his daughters in the 1930s and 1940s. He initially envisioned building a tourist attraction adjacent to his studios in Burbank to entertain fans who wished to visit; however, he soon realized that the proposed site was too small. After hiring a consultant to help him determine an appropriate site for his project, Disney bought a 160-acre (65 ha) site near Anaheim in 1953. Construction began in 1954 and the park was unveiled during a special televised press event on the ABC Television Network on July 17, 1955.

Since its opening, Disneyland has undergone expansions and major renovations, including the addition of New Orleans Square in 1966, Bear Country (now Critter Country) in 1972, Mickey's Toontown in 1993, and Star Wars: Galaxy's Edge in 2019. Opened in 2001, Disney California Adventure Park was built on the site of Disneyland's original parking lot.

---

* https://en.wikipedia.org/wiki/Disneyland

Disneyland는 1955년 7월 17일 개장한 Disneyland Resort의 두 개의 테마 파크 중 첫 번째 테마 파크로서, Walt Disney의 직접적인 감독 하에 설계되고 완성된 유일한 테마 파크이다. Walt Disney는 1930년대와 1940년대 딸들과 함께 다양한 놀이 공원을 방문한 후 Disneyland의 개념을 생각했고, 처음에는 방문하고 싶어 하는 팬들을 즐겁게 하기 위해 Burbank에 있는 자신의 스튜디오에 인접한 곳에 관광 명소를 짓는 것을 상상했지만, 곧 그 장소가 너무 작다는 것을 깨닫는다. 그는 자신의 프로젝트에 적합한 장소를 결정하기 위해 컨설턴트를 고용하였고, 1953년 Anaheim근처에서 160 에이커의 부지를 구입했다. 1954년 Disneyland 건설이 시작되었으며, 1955년 7월 17일 ABC Television Network에서 공개되었다.

Smart Vocabulary

supervision: 관리, 감독
property: 재산, 자산; 소유물(지)
expand: 펴다, 펼치다; 넓히다, 확장(확대)하다
come up with: (해답 등을) 찾아내다; 생각해내다
adjacent: 접근한, 인접한, 부근의
appropriate: (…에) 적합한, 적절(적당)한
undergo: 경험하다, 겪다

17. Universal Studios Hollywood *

Universal Studios Hollywood is a film studio and theme park in the San Fernando Valley area of Los Angeles County, California. About 70% of the studio lies within the unincorporated county island known as Universal City while the rest lies within the city limits of Los Angeles, California. It is one of the oldest and most famous Hollywood film studios still in use. Its official marketing headline is "The Entertainment Capital of LA". It was initially created to offer tours of the real Universal Studios sets and is the first of many full-fledged Universal Studios Theme Parks located across the world.

Outside the theme park, a new, all-digital facility near the Universal Pictures backlot was built in an effort to merge all of NBCUniversal's West Coast operations into one area. As a result, the current home for KNBC, KVEA and NBC News with Telemundo Los Angeles Bureaus with new digital facility is on the Universal lot formerly occupied by Technicolor SA. Universal City includes hotels Universal Hilton & Towers, the Sheraton Universal Hotel, and Universal CityWalk, which offers a collection of shops, restaurants, an 18-screen Universal Cinema and a seven-story IMAX theater. In 2017, the park hosted 9,056,000 guests, ranking it 15th in the world and 9th among North American parks.

---

* https://en.wikipedia.org/wiki/Universal_Studios_Hollywood

Universal Studios Hollywood는 Los Angeles County의 San Fernando Valley 지역에 있는 영화 스튜디오이자 테마 파크이다. Universal Studios는 여전히 사용 중인 가장 오래 되고 유명한 Hollywood 영화 스튜디오 중 하나이며, 공식적인 마케팅 제목은 "The Entertainment Capital of LA"이다.

Smart Vocabulary

unincorporated: 합병되지 않은; 법인 조직이 아닌
full-fledged: 자격이 충분한; 어엿한, 훌륭한
backlot: 촬영소가 그 근처에 소유하고 있는 야외 촬영 용지

18. Silicon Valley *

Silicon Valley is a region in the southern part of the San Francisco Bay Area in Northern California that serves as a global center for high technology, innovation, and social media. It corresponds roughly to the geographical Santa Clara Valley, although its boundaries have increased in recent decades. San Jose is the Valley's largest city, the third-largest in California, and the tenth-largest in the United States. Other major Silicon Valley cities include Palo Alto, Menlo Park, Redwood City, Cupertino, Santa Clara, Mountain View, and Sunnyvale. The San Jose Metropolitan Area has the third-highest GDP per capita in the world (after Zurich, Switzerland and Oslo, Norway), according to the Brookings Institution.

The word "silicon" in the name originally referred to the large number of innovators and manufacturers in the region specializing in silicon-based MOS transistors and integrated circuit chips. The area is now home to many of the world's largest high-tech corporations, including the headquarters of more than 30 businesses in the Fortune 1000, and thousands of startup companies. Silicon Valley also accounts for one-third of all of the venture capital investment in the United States, which has helped it to become a leading hub and startup ecosystem for high-tech innovation and scientific development. It was in Silicon Valley that the silicon-based integrated circuit, the microprocessor, and the microcomputer, among other technologies, were developed. As of 2013, the region employed about a quarter of a million information technology workers.

---

* https://en.wikipedia.org/wiki/Silicon_Valley

Silicon Valley는 Northern California에서 San Francisco Bay Area의 남쪽 지역으로서 첨단 기술, 혁신, 소셜 미디어의 글로벌 센터 역할을 한다. 최근 몇 십년간 Silicon Valley의 경계가 증가했음에도 불구하고, 그것은 지리적으로 Santa Clara Valley와 대략 일치한다. "silicon"이라는 단어는 원래 실리콘 기반의 MOS 트랜지스터와 집적 회로 칩을 전문으로 하는 지역의 많은 혁신자들과 제조업체들을 가리킨다. 이 지역은 Fortune지 선정 1000대 기업 중 30개 이상 기업의 본사와 수천 개의 신생 기업을 포함해서 세계에서 가장 큰 첨단 기술 기업들의 본거지이다.

Smart Vocabulary

correspond: 일치하다, 부합하다
geographical: 지리학(상)의, 지리(학)적인
boundary: 경계(선)
per capita: 1인당
integrated circuit: 집적회로

19. Grand Canyon *

The Grand Canyon is a steep-sided canyon carved by the Colorado River in Arizona, United States. The Grand Canyon is 277 miles (446 km) long, up to 18 miles (29 km) wide and attains a depth of over a mile (6,093 feet or 1,857 meters).

The canyon and adjacent rim are contained within Grand Canyon National Park, the Kaibab National Forest, Grand Canyon-Parashant National Monument, the Hualapai Indian Reservation, the Havasupai Indian Reservation and the Navajo Nation. President Theodore Roosevelt was a major proponent of preservation of the Grand Canyon area, and visited it on numerous occasions to hunt and enjoy the scenery.

Nearly two billion years of Earth's geological history have been exposed as the Colorado River and its tributaries cut their channels through layer after layer of rock while the Colorado Plateau was uplifted. While some aspects about the history of incision of the canyon are debated by geologists, several recent studies support the hypothesis that the Colorado River established its course through the area about 5 to 6 million years ago. Since that time, the Colorado River has driven the down-cutting of the tributaries and retreat of the cliffs, simultaneously deepening and widening the canyon.

For thousands of years, the area has been continuously inhabited by Native Americans, who built settlements within the canyon and its many caves. The Pueblo people considered the Grand Canyon a holy site, and made pilgrimages to it.

---

* https://en.wikipedia.org/wiki/Grand_Canyon

The Grand Canyon은 Arizona주의 북서쪽에 있는 협곡으로 거의 20억 년 동안의 지구의 지질학의 역사를 보여주며 South Rim과 North Rim으로 나눌 수 있다. Grand Canyon National Park는 1908년 미국에서 열다섯 번째로 국립공원에 지정되고, 1979년 UNESCO에 의해 World Heritage Site에 등재된다.

Smart Vocabulary

canyon: (개울이 흐르는 깊은) 협곡
steep: 가파른, 깎아지른 듯한
adjacent: 인접한, 부근의
rim: 가장자리, 테
reservation: 인디언 보호 거주지
proponent: 제안자, 옹호자
geological: 지질학(상)의; 지질의
tributary: (강의) 지류
plateau: 고원, 대지(臺地); (심해 밑의) 해대(海臺)
uplift: 올리다, 들어올리다
incision: 칼(벤)자국을 내기, 베기; 새김; 칼(벤)자국; 『의학』 쨈, 절개
geologist: 지질학자
hypothesis: 가설, 가정, 전제
retreat: 퇴각, 퇴거
simultaneously: 동시에; 일제히
inhabit: (…에) 살다, 거주하다, 서식하다

20. Niagara Falls [*]

Niagara Falls is a group of three waterfalls at the southern end of Niagara Gorge, between the Canadian province of Ontario and the US state of New York. The largest is Horseshoe Falls, also known as Canadian Falls, which straddles the international border between Canada and the United States. The smaller American Falls and Bridal Veil Falls lie entirely within the United States. Bridal Veil Falls are separated from Horseshoe Falls by Goat Island and from American Falls by Luna Island.

Located on the Niagara River, which drains Lake Erie into Lake Ontario, the combined falls have the highest flow rate of any waterfall in North America that has a vertical drop of more than 50 metres (160 ft). During peak daytime tourist hours, more than 168,000 m^3 (six million cubic feet) of water goes over the crest of the falls every minute. Horseshoe Falls is the most powerful waterfall in North America, as measured by flow rate.

The falls are 27 kilometres (17 mi) north-northwest of Buffalo, New York, and 121 kilometres (75 mi) south-southeast of Toronto, between the twin cities of Niagara Falls, Ontario, and Niagara Falls, New York. Niagara Falls was formed when glaciers receded at the end of the Wisconsin glaciation (the last ice age), and water from the newly formed Great Lakes carved a path through the Niagara Escarpment en route to the Atlantic Ocean.

Niagara Falls is famed both for its beauty and as a valuable source of hydroelectric power. Balancing recreational, commercial, and industrial uses has been a challenge for the stewards of the falls since the 19th century.

---

[*] https://en.wikipedia.org/wiki/Niagara_Falls

Niagara Falls는 캐나다의 Ontario주와 미국의 New York주의 국경선에 위치한 Niagara Gorge 남쪽의 세 개의 폭포, 즉 Goat Island를 기준으로 동쪽은 American Falls와 Bridal Veil Falls, 왼쪽은 캐나다의 Horseshoe Falls로 이루어져 있다.

Smart Vocabulary

gorge: 골짜기(ravine)
horseshoe: 편자, U 자 형의 물건
straddle: 가랑이를 벌리다, 다리를 벌리고 서다
drain: …에서 배수(방수)하다, …의 물을 빼내다
vertical: 수직의
crest: 볏, 꼭대기
recede: 물러나다, 퇴각하다; 멀어지다
glaciation: 빙하 작용
escarpment: 가파른 경사지; (일반적)급사면
en route: 도중에; 도중의
hydroelectric: 수력 전기의

21. Yosemite National Park *

Yosemite National Park is an American national park located in the western Sierra Nevada of Central California, bounded on the southeast by Sierra National Forest and on the northwest by Stanislaus National Forest. The park is managed by the National Park Service and covers an area of 748,436 acres (1,169 sq mi; 3,029 km^2) and sits in four counties: centered in Tuolumne and Mariposa, extending north and east to Mono and south to Madera County. Designated a World Heritage site in 1984, Yosemite is internationally recognized for its granite cliffs, waterfalls, clear streams, giant sequoia groves, lakes, mountains, meadows, glaciers, and biological diversity. Almost 95% of the park is designated wilderness.

On average, about four million people visit Yosemite each year, and most spend the majority of their time in the seven square miles (18 km^2) of Yosemite Valley. The park set a visitation record in 2016, surpassing five million visitors for the first time in its history. Yosemite was central to the development of the national park idea. Galen Clark and others lobbied to protect Yosemite Valley from development, ultimately leading to President Abraham Lincoln's signing the Yosemite Grant in 1864. John Muir led a successful movement to have Congress establish a larger national park by 1890, one which encompassed the valley and its surrounding mountains and forests, paving the way for the National Park System.

---

* https://en.wikipedia.org/wiki/Yosemite_National_Park

Yosemite National Park는 Central California의 Sierra Nevada 산맥의 서쪽에 위치한 국립공원으로 U자형의 계곡, 화강암 절벽, 미국에서 가장 높은 Yosemite 폭포와 면사포 폭포(Bridal Veil Fall)를 포함한 많은 폭포, 세쿼이아 숲, 300개 이상의 호수, 초원, 빙하와 생물학적인 다양성을 국제적으로 인정받고 있다. Yosemite는 1890년 국립공원으로 지정되고, 1984년 유네스코의 세계 자연유산에 등재된다.

Smart Vocabulary

bound: 인접하다, 접경하다(on)
granite: 화강암
sequoia: 세쿼이아(미국 캘리포니아 주산(州產) 삼나무과의 거목(巨木))
grove: 작은 숲
glacier: 빙하
biological: 생물학(상)의
diversity: 다양성, 변화(variety)
wilderness: 황야, 미개지, 사람이 살지 않는 땅
surpass: …보다 낫다, …을 능가하다
encompass: 둘러[에워]싸다, 포위하다
pave the way for(to): …에의 길을 열다, …을 가능케 하다

22. Death Valley *

 Death Valley is a desert valley located in Eastern California, in the northern Mojave Desert bordering the Great Basin Desert. It is one of the hottest places in the world along with deserts in the Middle East.

 Death Valley's Badwater Basin is the point of the lowest elevation in North America, at 282 feet (86 m) below sea level. This point is 84.6 miles (136.2 km) east-southeast of Mount Whitney, the highest point in the contiguous United States, with an elevation of 14,505 feet (4,421 m). On the afternoon of July 10, 1913, the United States Weather Bureau recorded a high temperature of 134 °F (56.7 °C) at Furnace Creek in Death Valley. This temperature stands as the highest ambient air temperature ever recorded at the surface of the Earth.

---

* https://en.wikipedia.org/wiki/Death_Valley

Death Valley는 Eastern California에 위치한 사막 계곡으로서, Great Basin Desert와 인접한 Mojave Desert에 있다. 이곳은 Middle East의 사막과 함께 세계에서 가장 더운 곳 중 하나인데, 1913년 7월 10일 오후, 미국 Weather Bureau는 Death Valley의 계곡의 Furnace Creek에서 134°F(56.7 °C)의 고온을 기록했다.

Smart Vocabulary

basin: 분지
border: 접경하다, 접하다
elevation: 높이, 고도
contiguous: 인접한, 근접한
ambient: 주위의, 환경의
constitute: 구성하다, 조직하다

23. Facebook *

Facebook is an American online social media and social networking service based in Menlo Park, California and a flagship service of the namesake company Facebook, Inc. It was founded by Mark Zuckerberg, along with fellow Harvard College students and roommates Eduardo Saverin, Andrew McCollum, Dustin Moskovitz and Chris Hughes.

The founders initially limited Facebook membership to Harvard students. Membership was expanded to Ivy League universities, MIT, and higher education institutions in the Boston area, then various other universities, and lastly high school students. Since 2006, anyone who claims to be at least 13 years old has been allowed to become a registered user of Facebook, though this may vary depending on local laws. The name comes from the face book directories often given to American university students.

The Facebook service can be accessed from devices with Internet connectivity, such as personal computers, tablets and smartphones. After registering, users can create a profile revealing information about themselves. They can post text, photos and multimedia which is shared with any other users that have agreed to be their "friend", or, with a different privacy setting, with any reader. Users can also use various embedded apps, join common-interest groups, buy and sell items or services on Marketplace, and receive notifications of their Facebook friends' activities and activities of Facebook pages they follow. Facebook claimed that it had more than 2.3 billion monthly active users as of December 2018.

---

* https://en.wikipedia.org/wiki/Facebook

Facebook은 California 주 Menlo Park에 본사를 둔 온라인 소셜 미디어 및 소셜 네트워킹 서비스로서 Mark Zuckerberg가 Harvard 대학의 동료 학생들인 Eduardo Saverin, Andrew McCollum, Dustin Moskovitz, Chris Hughes와 함께 설립했다. 그들은 처음에 Facebook 회원 자격을 Harvard 대학 학생들로 제한했으나 Ivy League 대학, MIT, 보스턴 지역의 고등 교육 기관, 다른 대학, 마지막으로 고등학생으로까지 확대했다.

Smart Vocabulary

flagship: 기함; (일련의 것 중) 최고의 것
namesake: 이름이 같은 사람(것)
directory: 주소 성명록, 인명부; 전화번호부
access: 접근하다
connectivity: 연결(성)
embed: (물건을) 끼워 넣다, 묻다; (마음·기억 등에) 깊이 새겨 두다
notification: 통지, 통고, 고시

24. Twitter *

Twitter is an American microblogging and social networking service on which users post and interact with messages known as "tweets". Registered users can post, like, and retweet tweets, but unregistered users can only read them. Users access Twitter through its website interface, through Short Message Service (SMS) or its mobile-device application software ("app"). Twitter, Inc. is based in San Francisco, California, and has more than 25 offices around the world. Tweets were originally restricted to 140 characters, but was doubled to 280 for non-Asian languages in November 2017.

Twitter was created in March 2006 by Jack Dorsey, Noah Glass, Biz Stone, and Evan Williams, launched in July of that year. The service rapidly gained worldwide popularity. In 2012, more than 100 million users posted 340 million tweets a day, and the service handled an average of 1.6 billion search queries per day. In 2013, it was one of the ten most-visited websites and has been described as "the SMS of the Internet". As of 2018, Twitter had more than 321 million monthly active users.

---

* https://en.wikipedia.org/wiki/Twitter

Twitter는 2006년 3월에 Jack Dorsey, Noah Glass, Biz Stone, and Evan William이 만들어 7월에 출시된 마이크로블로깅 및 소셜 네트워킹 서비스로서, 본사는 California 주 San Francisco에 있다. 사용자는 웹사이트 인터페이스, Short Message Service 또는 app을 통해 Twitter에 접근할 수 있다. 원래 Twitter는 140자로 제한되었으나, 2017년 11월 아시아 이외의 언어에서는 280자까지 두 배로 늘어났다.

Smart Vocabulary

microblogging: 짤막한 메시지나 영상 등을 인터넷에 정기적으로 올리는 활동
interact: 상호 작용하다, 서로 영향을 주다
interface: 중간면, 접촉면; (상호) 작용을 미치는 영역; 상호 작용(전달)의 수단
restrict: 제한하다, 한정하다
query: 질문(inquiry), 의문

25. NASA *

The National Aeronautics and Space Administration (NASA) is an independent agency of the United States Federal Government responsible for the civilian space program, as well as aeronautics and aerospace research.

NASA was established in 1958, succeeding the National Advisory Committee for Aeronautics (NACA). The new agency was to have a distinctly civilian orientation, encouraging peaceful applications in space science. Since its establishment, most US space exploration efforts have been led by NASA, including the Apollo Moon landing missions, the Skylab space station, and later the Space Shuttle. NASA is supporting the International Space Station and is overseeing the development of the Orion Multi-Purpose Crew Vehicle, the Space Launch System and Commercial Crew vehicles. The agency is also responsible for the Launch Services Program which provides oversight of launch operations and countdown management for uncrewed NASA launches.

NASA science is focused on better understanding Earth through the Earth Observing System; advancing heliophysics through the efforts of the Science Mission Directorate's Heliophysics Research Program; exploring bodies throughout the Solar System with advanced robotic spacecraft missions such as New Horizons; and researching astrophysics topics, such as the Big Bang, through the Great Observatories and associated programs.

---

* https://en.wikipedia.org/wiki/NASA

NASA(미항공우주국)는 1958년 NACA(미항공자문위원회)의 뒤를 이어 설립되었으며, 항공학과 항공 우주 연구 뿐 아니라 민간 우주 프로그램을 담당하는 미국 연방 정부의 독립 기관이다. NASA는 분명히 민간 주도로 우주 과학의 평화적인 적용을 장려하려고 했으며, 이 기관의 설립 이래 Apollo 달 착륙 임무, Skylab 우주 정거장, 그리고 Space Shuttle을 포함한 대부분의 미국 우주 탐험 노력들을 이끌게 된다. 또한 NASA는 International Space Station을 지원하고, Orion Multi-Purpose Crew Vehicle, Space Launch System, Commercial Crew 차량의 개발을 감독하고 있다. NASA는 발사 작업을 감독하고 무인 NASA 발사에 대한 카운트다운 관리를 제공하는 Launch Services Program을 책임진다.

Smart Vocabulary

aeronautics: pl.(단수취급)항공학[술]
aerospace: 우주 공간; 항공 우주 산업; 항공 우주 과학
succeed: …에 계속되다, …에 대신하다
oversee: 감독하다
oversight: 감독, 감시, 단속, 관리
launch: 발진, 발사; 진수(식)진수대
heliophysics: 태양 자체와 태양과 지구, 다른 항성계와의 상호작용 등을 연구하는 학문
directorate: director의 직, 관리직
spacecraft: 우주선(spaceship)
astrophysics: pl.(단수취급)천체 물리학
Big Bang: (우주 생성 때의) 대폭발

26. FBI *

The Federal Bureau of Investigation (FBI) is the domestic intelligence and security service of the United States and its principal federal law enforcement agency. Operating under the jurisdiction of the United States Department of Justice, the FBI is also a member of the U.S. Intelligence Community and reports to both the Attorney General and the Director of National Intelligence. A leading U.S. counter-terrorism, counterintelligence, and criminal investigative organization, the FBI has jurisdiction over violations of more than 200 categories of federal crimes.

Although many of the FBI's functions are unique, its activities in support of national security are comparable to those of the British MI5 and the Russian FSB. Unlike the Central Intelligence Agency (CIA), which has no law enforcement authority and is focused on intelligence collection abroad, the FBI is primarily a domestic agency, maintaining 56 field offices in major cities throughout the United States, and more than 400 resident agencies in smaller cities and areas across the nation. At an FBI field office, a senior-level FBI officer concurrently serves as the representative of the Director of National Intelligence.

---

* https://en.wikipedia.org/wiki/Federal_Bureau_of_Investigation

The Federal Bureau of Investigation (FBI)은 1908년 설립된 미국의 국내 정보 및 보안 서비스를 담당하고 주요 연방 법률을 집행한다. FBI는 Department of Justice의 관할 하에 대테러, 방첩 활동, 범죄 수사를 하는 기관으로서 법무부 장관과 국가 정보 국장에게 보고한다. FBI의 기능이 독특하지만, 국가 안보를 위한 활동은 영국의 MI5나 러시아의 FSB와 비교할 수 있다.

Smart Vocabulary

investigation: 조사, 연구, 수사
enforcement: (법률의) 시행, 집행
jurisdiction: 재판권, 사법권; 관할권; 권한, 지배
Department of Justice: 법무부
counterintelligence: 방첩 활동
violation: 위반
in support of …의 원조(변호)로, …을 옹호하여
Attorney General: 《美》(연방 정부의) 법무 장관; 《美》(각 주의) 검찰 총장
authority: 권한
concurrently: 동시에, 함께, 겸임하여
representative: 대표자, 대행자, 대리인

27. CIA *

The Central Intelligence Agency (CIA) is a civilian foreign intelligence service of the federal government of the United States, tasked with gathering, processing, and analyzing national security information from around the world, primarily through the use of human intelligence (HUMINT). As one of the principal members of the United States Intelligence Community (IC), the CIA reports to the Director of National Intelligence and is primarily focused on providing intelligence for the President and Cabinet of the United States.

Unlike the Federal Bureau of Investigation (FBI), which is a domestic security service, the CIA has no law enforcement function and is mainly focused on overseas intelligence gathering, with only limited domestic intelligence collection. Though it is not the only agency of the federal government of the United States specializing in HUMINT, the CIA serves as the national manager for coordination of HUMINT activities across the U.S. intelligence community. Moreover, the CIA is the only agency authorized by law to carry out and oversee covert action at the behest of the President. It exerts foreign political influence through its tactical divisions, such as the Special Activities Center. The CIA was also instrumental in establishing intelligence services in several U.S. allied countries, such as Germany's BND.

---

* https://en.wikipedia.org/wiki/Central_Intelligence_Agency

The Central Intelligence Agency (CIA)는 미국 연방 정부의 민간 해외 정보기관으로 전 세계로부터 국가 안보 정보를 수집하고 처리하며 분석하는 업무를 수행한다. 국내 보안 기관인 FBI와는 달리, CIA는 법을 집행하는 기능이 없고 주로 해외 정보를 수집하는 활동에 집중하면서 단지 제한된 국내 정보를 수집할 뿐이다. 또한 CIA는 대통령의 명령에 따라 비밀 작전을 수행하고 감독하는 법적 권한을 가진 유일한 기관이다.

Smart Vocabulary

Cabinet: 내각
enforcement: (법률의) 시행, 집행
coordination: 조정
covert: 비밀의, 암암리의, 은밀한
at the behest of: ~의 명령을 따라서
exert: 발휘하다, 쓰다
tactical: 전술상의; 책략(술책)이 능란한
division: 구분, 부분; 구(區), 부(部)
instrumental: 유효한, 수단이 되는, 쓸모 있는
concurrently: 동시에, 함께, 겸임하여
ally: 동맹(결연 · 연합 · 제휴)하게 하다

28. Harvard University *

Harvard University is a private Ivy League research university in Cambridge, Massachusetts, with about 6,800 undergraduate students and about 14,000 postgraduate students. Established in 1636 and named for its first benefactor, clergyman John Harvard, Harvard is the United States' oldest institution of higher learning. Its history, influence, wealth, and academic reputation have made it one of the most prestigious universities in the world.

The Harvard Corporation, chartered in 1650, is the governing body of Harvard. In its early years, Harvard College primarily trained Congregational and Unitarian clergy, although it has never been formally affiliated with any denomination. Its curriculum and student body were gradually secularized during the 18th century, and by the 19th century, Harvard had emerged as the central cultural establishment among Boston elites. Following the American Civil War, President Charles W. Eliot's long tenure (1869-1909) transformed the college and affiliated professional schools into a modern research university; Harvard was a founding member of the Association of American Universities in 1900. A. Lawrence Lowell, who succeeded Eliot, further reformed the undergraduate curriculum and undertook aggressive expansion of Harvard's land holdings and physical campus. James Bryant Conant led the university through the Great Depression and World War II; he began to liberalize admissions after the war.

---

* https://en.wikipedia.org/wiki/Harvard_University

Harvard University는 1636년 John Harvard 목사의 후원으로 Massachusetts 주 Cambridge에 설립되었으며, 약 6,800명의 학부생과 14,000명의 대학원생이 다니고 있다. Harvard University는 미국에서 가장 오래된 고등 교육 기관으로서 이 대학의 역사, 영향력, 부, 그리고 학문적 명성으로 인해 세계에서 가장 권위 있는 대학 중 하나가 되었다. Ivy League는 북동부 지역의 8개 사립대학으로 Harvard를 비롯하여 Yale, Pennsylvania, Princeton, Columbia, Brown, Dartmouth, Cornell 대학교이다.

Smart Vocabulary

undergraduate: 대학 학부 재학생, 대학생(의)
postgraduate: 대학원 학생; 대학원의
benefactor: 후원자; 기증(기부)자
clergyman: 성직자
prestigious: 명성 있는; 유명한
corporation: 법인, 협회, 사단 법인
charter: (회사 등을) 설립하다
Congregational: (C-) 조합(組合) 교회의
Unitarian: 유니테리언교도《삼위일체를 인정하지 않음》; 유니테리언교의
affiliate: 관계(가입)하다; 제휴하다, 손잡다
denomination: 교단, 교파
secularize: 세속화하다; (교육을) 종교에서 분리하다
tenure: 재직기간, 임기
undertake: 떠맡다, ⋯의 책임을 지다
aggressive: 적극적인; 과감한

29. Massachusetts Institute of Technology [*]

Massachusetts Institute of Technology (MIT) is a private research university in Cambridge, Massachusetts. The Institute is a land-grant, sea-grant, and space-grant university, with an urban campus that extends more than a mile (1.6 km) alongside the Charles River. The Institute also encompasses a number of major off-campus facilities such as the MIT Lincoln Laboratory, the Bates Center, and the Haystack Observatory, as well as affiliated laboratories such as the Broad and Whitehead Institutes. Founded in 1861 in response to the increasing industrialization of the United States, MIT adopted a European polytechnic university model and stressed laboratory instruction in applied science and engineering. It has since played a key role in the development of many aspects of modern science, engineering, mathematics, and technology, and is widely known for its innovation and academic strength, making it one of the most prestigious institutions of higher learning in the world.

---

[*] https://en.wikipedia.org/wiki/Massachusetts_Institute_of_Technology

Massachusetts Institute of Technology (MIT)는 1861년 미국의 산업화가 증가함에 따라 설립되었으며, Massachusetts 주 Cambridge에 위치한 사립 연구 대학이다. MIT는 Charles River를 따라 1.6km이상 뻗어 있으며 MIT Lincoln Laboratory, the Bates Center, the Haystack Observatory와 같은 많은 시설과 the Broad and Whitehead Institutes와 같은 제휴 연구소를 포함하고 있다. MIT는 설립된 이래 유럽의 종합 과학 기술 대학 모델을 채택했고 응용과학과 공학 분야에서 실험실 교육을 강조했고, 현대 과학, 공학, 수학, 기술 분야를 발전시키는 데 중요한 역할을 했고 혁신과 학문적인 힘으로 널리 알려져 있다.

Smart Vocabulary

land-grant: 무상 토지 불하
sea-grant college: 미(국립) 고등 해양 연구소
encompass: 둘러(에워)싸다; 포함하다
laboratory: 실험실; 연구소(실)
observatory: 천문(기상, 관상)대; 전망대
polytechnic: 종합(과학) 기술의

30. Stanford University [*]

Stanford University, officially Leland Stanford Junior University, is a private research university in Stanford, California. Stanford is known for its academic achievements, wealth, close proximity to Silicon Valley, and selectivity; it ranks as one of the world's top universities.

The university was founded in 1885 by Leland and Jane Stanford in memory of their only child, Leland Stanford Jr., who had died of typhoid fever at age 15 the previous year. Stanford was a U.S. Senator and former Governor of California who made his fortune as a railroad tycoon. The school admitted its first students on October 1, 1891, as a coeducational and non-denominational institution.

Stanford University struggled financially after the death of Leland Stanford in 1893 and again after much of the campus was damaged by the 1906 San Francisco earthquake. Following World War II, Provost Frederick Terman supported faculty and graduates' entrepreneurialism to build self-sufficient local industry in what would later be known as Silicon Valley. The university is also one of the top fundraising institutions in the country, becoming the first school to raise more than a billion dollars in a year.

---

[*] https://en.wikipedia.org/wiki/Stanford_University

Stanford University는 공식적으로 Leland Stanford Junior University이며, California 주 Stanford에 있는 사립 연구 대학이다. Stanford University는 1885년 Leland and Jane Stanford가 한 해 전 15세에 장티푸스로 사망한 외동아들인 Leland Stanford Jr.를 기념하기 위해 설립되었다. Stanford는 철도 업계 거물로 부자가 되고, 상원 의원이자 전 California 주지사였으며, Stanford University는 1891년 10월 1일 남녀 공학과 특정 종교에 관계가 없는 대학으로 첫 학생들을 입학시켰다.

Smart Vocabulary

proximity: 근접, 가까움
in memory of: …의 기념으로
typhoid fever: 장티푸스
make a fortune: 재산을 모으다, 부자가 되다
tycoon: (재계의) 거물
coeducational: 남녀 공학의
non-denominational: 특정 종교에 관계가 없는
entrepreneurialism: 기업가 정신[주의]
self-sufficient: 자급(자족)할 수 있는, 경제적으로 자립한

31. GM *

General Motors Company, commonly referred to as General Motors (GM), is an American multinational corporation headquartered in Detroit that designs, manufactures, markets, and distributes vehicles and vehicle parts, and sells financial services, with global headquarters in Detroit's Renaissance Center. It was originally founded by William C. Durant on September 16, 1908 as a holding company. The company is the largest American automobile manufacturer, and one of the world's largest. As of 2019, General Motors is ranked #13 on the Fortune 500 rankings of the largest United States corporations by total revenue.

General Motors manufactures vehicles in 15 countries; its core automobile brands include Chevrolet, Buick, GMC, and Cadillac. It also either owns or holds a significant stake in foreign brands such as Holden, Wuling, Baojun, and Jiefang. Annual worldwide sales volume reached a milestone of 10 million vehicles in 2016.

---

* https://en.wikipedia.org/wiki/General_Motors

General Motors Company는 1908년 9월 16일 William C. Durant가 지주 회사로 설립했으며, 자동차와 차 부품을 설계, 제조, 유통하고 금융 서비스를 판매하는 미국 다국적 기업으로서 Detroit에 본사가 있다. GM은 15개국에서 자동차를 제조하며, 핵심 자동차 브랜드는 Chevrolet, Buick, GMC, and Cadillac이다.

Smart Vocabulary

refer to ... as __ : …을 —의 이름으로 부르다(—로 칭하다)
holding company: 지주 회사
stake: 주(株)의 보유분
milestone: 이정표; (인생·역사 따위의) 중대 시점, 획기적인 사건

32. Ford *

Ford Motor Company, commonly known as Ford, is an American multinational automaker that has its main headquarters in Dearborn, Michigan, a suburb of Detroit. It was founded by Henry Ford and incorporated on June 16, 1903. The company sells automobiles and commercial vehicles under the Ford brand, and most luxury cars under the Lincoln brand. Ford also owns Brazilian SUV manufacturer Troller, an 8% stake in Aston Martin of the United Kingdom and a 32% stake in Jiangling Motors. It also has joint-ventures in China (Changan Ford), Taiwan (Ford Lio Ho), Thailand (AutoAlliance Thailand), Turkey (Ford Otosan), and Russia (Ford Sollers). The company is listed on the New York Stock Exchange and is controlled by the Ford family; they have minority ownership but the majority of the voting power.

Ford introduced methods for large-scale manufacturing of cars and large-scale management of an industrial workforce using elaborately engineered manufacturing sequences typified by moving assembly lines; by 1914, these methods were known around the world as Fordism. Ford's former UK subsidiaries Jaguar and Land Rover, acquired in 1989 and 2000 respectively, were sold to the Indian automaker Tata Motors in March 2008. Ford owned the Swedish automaker Volvo from 1999 to 2010. In 2011, Ford discontinued the Mercury brand, under which it had marketed entry-level luxury cars in the United States, Canada, Mexico, and the Middle East since 1938.

---

* https://en.wikipedia.org/wiki/Ford_Motor_Company

Ford Motor Company는 1903년 6월 16일 Henry Ford가 설립했고, Michigan 주 Dearborn에 본사를 두고 있는 미국 제2의 다국적 자동차 회사이다. Ford는 자동차와 상업용 자동차를 Ford 브랜드로 판매하고, 대부분의 고급차는 Lincoln 브랜드로 판매한다. Ford는 자동차를 대량 생산하는 방법과 산업 인력을 대규모로 관리하는 방법을 도입했으며, 1914년까지 이러한 방법은 전 세계적으로 Fordism으로 알려졌다.

Smart Vocabulary

suburb: 교외, 근교
incorporate: 주식회사로 하다
stake: 주(株)의 보유분
elaborately: 공들여, 애써서, 정교하게
sequence: 연속, 연쇄, 계속; 순서, 차례
typify: 대표하다; 유형화하다
subsidiary: 자회사
respectively: 각자, 각각, 제각기

33. NBA *

The National Basketball Association (NBA) is a men's professional basketball league in North America, composed of 30 teams (29 in the United States and 1 in Canada). It is one of the four major professional sports leagues in the United States and Canada, and is widely considered to be the premier men's professional basketball league in the world.

The league was founded in New York City on June 6, 1946, as the Basketball Association of America (BAA). It changed its name to the National Basketball Association on August 3, 1949, after merging with the competing National Basketball League (NBL). The NBA's regular season runs from October to April, with each team playing 82 games. Its playoffs extend into June. As of 2015, NBA players are the world's best paid athletes by average annual salary per player.

---

* https://en.wikipedia.org/wiki/National_Basketball_Association

National Basketball Association (NBA)는 북미 지역의 남자 프로 농구 리그로서 미국 팀 29개, 캐나다 팀1개 총 30개 팀으로 구성되어 있다. NBA는 1946년 6월 6일 New York City에서 Basketball Association of America (BAA)로 설립되었고, 경쟁 관계였던 National Basketball League (NBL)와 합병한 후 1949년 8월 3일 전미농구협회(NBL)로 이름을 변경했다. NBA의 정규 시즌은 10월부터 4월까지 열리며, 각 팀은 82번의 경기를 하고, 시즌 종료 후 우승 결정전 시리즈는 6월까지 계속된다.

Smart Vocabulary

premier: 첫째의, 수위의; 최초의
merge: 합병하다
playoff: (시즌 종료 후의) 우승 결정전 시리즈
extend: 연장하다, 늘이다
athlete: 운동선수

34. CNN *

CNN (Cable News Network) is an American news-based pay television channel owned by AT&T's WarnerMedia. CNN was founded in 1980 by American media proprietor Ted Turner as a 24-hour cable news channel. Upon its launch in 1980, CNN was the first television channel to provide 24-hour news coverage and was the first all-news television channel in the United States.

While the news channel has numerous affiliates, CNN primarily broadcasts from 30 Hudson Yards in New York City, and studios in Washington, D.C. and Los Angeles. Its headquarters at the CNN Center in Atlanta is only used for weekend programming. CNN is sometimes referred to as CNN/U.S. (or CNN Domestic) to distinguish the U.S. channel from its international sister network, CNN International.

The network is known for its dramatic live coverage of breaking news, some of which has drawn criticism as overly sensationalistic, and for its efforts to be nonpartisan, which have led to accusations of false balance.

As of September 2018, CNN has 90.1 million television households as subscribers (97.7% of households with cable) in the United States.

Globally, CNN programming airs through CNN International, which can be seen by viewers in over 212 countries and territories.

---

* https://en.wikipedia.org/wiki/CNN

CNN은 1980년 6월 미국의 미디어 경영자인 Ted Turner가 설립하였으며, 본사는 Georgia 주 Atlanta에 있다. AT&T의 WarnerMedia가 소유한 CNN은 24시간 뉴스만을 방송하는 텔레비전 채널로서 광고 수입으로 운영된다.

Smart Vocabulary

proprietor: 소유자; 경영자
coverage: 보도; 적용(통용, 보증) 범위.
affiliate: 가입자, 회원
refer: 언급하다
breaking news: 긴급뉴스
overly: 과도하게, 지나치게
nonpartisan: 당파에 속하지 않은 (사람), 무소속의 (사람)
accusation: 비난; 고발, 고소
subscriber: 신청자; 가입자
territory: 영토, 땅

35. Voice of America *

Voice of America (VOA) is a U.S. multimedia agency which serves as the United States non-government institution for non-military, external broadcasting. It is the largest U.S. international broadcaster. VOA produces digital, TV, and radio content in more than 40 languages which it distributes to affiliate stations around the globe. It is primarily viewed by foreign audiences, so VOA programming has an influence on public opinion abroad regarding the United States and its people.

VOA was established in 1942, and the VOA charter (Public Laws 94-350 and 103-415)[3] was signed into law in 1976 by President Gerald Ford. The charter contains its mission "to broadcast accurate, balanced, and comprehensive news and information to an international audience", and it defines the legally mandated standards in the VOA journalistic code.

VOA is headquartered in Washington, D.C., and overseen by the U.S. Agency for Global Media, an independent agency of the U.S. government. Funds are appropriated annually by Congress under the budget for embassies and consulates. In 2016, VOA broadcast an estimated 1,800 hours of radio and TV programming each week to approximately 236.6 million people worldwide with about 1,050 employees and a taxpayer-funded annual budget of US$ 218.5 million.

Some commentators consider Voice of America to be a form of propaganda. However, VOA's Best Practices Guide states that "The accuracy, quality and credibility of the Voice of America are its most important assets, and they rest on the audiences' perception of VOA as an objective and reliable source of U.S., regional and world news and information." Surveys show that 84% of VOA's audiences say they trust VOA to provide accurate and reliable information, and a similar percentage (84%) say that VOA helps them understand current events relevant to their lives.

---

* https://en.wikipedia.org/wiki/Voice_of_America

Voice of America는 미국의 비군사적이고 대외적인 방송을 위한 비정부 멀티미디어 기관이다. 1942년에 설립된 VOA는 미국에서 가장 큰 국제 방송사로서 전 세계 40개 이상의 언어로 디지털, TV 및 라디오 콘텐츠를 제작하고 배포한다. 1976년 Gerald Ford 대통령에 의해 법률로 서명된 VOA 헌장은 "정확하고 균형 잡힌 포괄적인 뉴스와 정보를 국제 청취자에게 방송하는 것"이라는 사명을 포함하고 있다.

Smart Vocabulary

affiliate: 가입자, 회원; 지부, 계열(자매) 회사; 가맹 계열방송국
charter: 헌장, (목적·강령 등의) 선언서
comprehensive: 포괄적인
mandate: …에게 위임하다; 명령(지령, 요구)하다
oversee: (작업 등을) 감독하다
appropriate: (어떤 목적에) 충당하다
consulate: 영사관
approximately: 대략, 대강
commentator: (시사)해설자
propaganda: 선전; (선전하는) 주의, 주장
credibility: 믿을 수 있음; 신용, 신뢰
asset: (회사·개인의) 자산, 재산
perception: 지각(작용); 인식
relevant: 관련된; 적절한

36. AP [*]

The Associated Press (AP) is an American not-for-profit news agency headquartered in New York City. Founded in 1846, it operates as a cooperative, unincorporated association. Its members are U.S. newspapers and broadcasters. The AP news report, distributed to its members and customers, is produced in English, Spanish and Arabic. The AP has earned 53 Pulitzer Prizes, including 31 for photography, since the award was established in 1917.

The AP has counted the vote in U.S. elections since 1848, including national, state and local races down to the legislative level in all 50 states, along with key ballot measures. The AP collects and verifies returns in every county, parish, city and town across the U.S., and declares winners in over 5,000 contests.

---

[*] https://en.wikipedia.org/wiki/Associated_Press

The Associated Press (AP)는 1848년 New York City에서 설립된 비영리 통신사로서 전 세계 언론사와 통신사에 뉴스와 사진을 제공한다. AP는 영국의 Reuters 통신, 프랑스의 Agence France-Presse (AFP)와 함께 세계 3대 통신사에 속한다.

Smart Vocabulary

news agency: 통신사
cooperative: 협력적인
unincorporated: 법인 조직이 아닌
association: 연합, 관련, 결합, 합동, 제휴
distribute: 배포하다, 배급하다
legislative: 입법(상)의; 입법부의
ballot: 투표; 투표용지
verify: 증명(입증, 실증, 확증)하다
return: (보통 pl.) 개표 보고
parish: 《주로 英》 본당(本堂), 교구(敎區)

37. Ted *

TED Conferences LLC (Technology, Entertainment, Design) is an American media organization that posts scripted speeches taped before live audiences, called "Talks", online for free distribution. Talks are accompanied by the slogan "ideas worth spreading". TED was conceived by Richard Saul Wurman, in February 1984, as a conference; it has been held annually since 1990. TED's early emphasis was on technology and design, consistent with its Silicon Valley origins. It has since broadened its perspective to include Talks on many scientific, cultural, political, and academic topics. It is owned and curated by Chris Anderson, a British-American businessman, through the Sapling Foundation.

The main TED conference is held annually in Vancouver, British Columbia, Canada at the Vancouver Convention Centre. Prior to 2014, the conference was held in Long Beach, California, United States. TED events are also held throughout North America and in Europe, Asia and Africa, offering live streaming of the talks. They address a wide range of topics within the research and practice of science and culture, often through storytelling. The speakers are given a maximum of 18 minutes to present their ideas in the most innovative and engaging ways they can.

Past speakers include Bill Clinton, Sean M. Carroll, Elon Musk, Ray Dalio, Cédric Villani, Stephen Hawking, Jane Goodall, Al Gore, Temple Grandin, Shahrukh Khan, Gordon Brown, David Cameron, Billy Graham, Richard Dawkins, Sam Harris, Bill Gates, Dolph Lundgren, Bob Weir, Shashi Tharoor, Bono, Larry Page and Sergey Brin, Leana Wen, Pope Francis, and many Nobel Prize winners. TED's current curator is Chris Anderson, a British-American businessman, computer journalist and magazine publisher.

---

* https://en.wikipedia.org/wiki/TED_(conference)

TED Conferences LLC는 온라인에서 무료로 배포되는 "Talks", 즉 청중 앞에서 녹음된 연설문을 게시하며, 이 "Talks"에는 "퍼뜨릴 가치가 있는 아이디어"라는 슬로건이 붙어 있다. TED는 1984년 2월 Richard Saul Wurman이 처음 구상했으며, 1990년부터 매년 개최되어 왔다. TED의 초기 강조점은 기술과 디자인이었지만, 이후 과학적, 문화적, 정치적, 학술적 주제를 포함하게 된다. TED에서 강연자들은 최대 18분 동안 그들이 할 수 있는 가장 혁신적이고 매력적인 방법으로 자신의 아이디어를 발표한다.

Smart Vocabulary

script: [대본을] 쓰다
distribution: 배포
accompany: …에 동반하다, …와 함께 가다
conceive: 마음에 품다; 착상하다; 생각하다
conference: 회의, 협의회
consistent: (…와) 일치(양립)하는; 조화된
perspective: 전망; 시각
a wide range of: 광범위한
innovative: 혁신적인
engaging: 마음을 끄는, 매력적인
curator: 관리자, 관장; 감독

38. Time *

Time is an American weekly news magazine and news website published in New York City. It was founded in 1923 and for many years it was run by its influential co-founder Henry Luce. A European edition (Time Europe, formerly known as Time Atlantic) is published in London and also covers the Middle East, Africa, and, since 2003, Latin America. An Asian edition (Time Asia) is based in Hong Kong. The South Pacific edition, which covers Australia, New Zealand, and the Pacific Islands, is based in Sydney. In December 2008, *Time* discontinued publishing a Canadian advertiser edition.

Time has the world's largest circulation for a weekly news magazine. The print edition has a readership of 26 million, 20 million of whom are based in the United States. In mid-2012, its circulation was over 3 million, which fell to 2 million by late 2017.

Formerly published by *Time* Inc., since November 2018 *Time* has been published by TIME USA, LLC, owned by Marc Benioff who acquired it from Meredith Corporation two months earlier.

---

* https://en.wikipedia.org/wiki/Time_(magazine)

Time magazine은 Yale Daily News의 사장과 편집자로 각각 일했던 Briton Hadden과 Henry Luce가 1923년 3월 3일 창간했으며, 미국에서 제일 먼저 발행된 시사 주간지이다. 그들은 처음에 그 잡지의 이름을 Facts 라고 불렀으며, 간결함을 강조하기 위해 바쁜 사람도 한 시간 내에 읽을 수 있게 만들었다. 그들은 *Time*이라고 이름을 바꾸며, "Take Time - It's Brief"라는 슬로건을 사용했다. *Time*은 London에서 발행되는 Time Europe을 비롯하여 Middle East, Africa, Latin America, Asia, South Pacific을 발행한다.

Smart Vocabulary

co-founder: 공동 창설(창립)자
Atlantic: (the ~) 대서양
discontinue: 그만두다, 중지하다
circulation: (서적·잡지 따위의) 발행 부수

39. Newsweek *

Newsweek is an American weekly news magazine founded in 1933. *Newsweek* was a widely distributed newsweekly through the 20th century, with many notable editors-in-chief throughout the years. *Newsweek* was acquired by The Washington Post Company in 1961, under whose ownership it remained until 2010. Between 2008 and 2012, *Newsweek* experienced financial difficulties, leading to the cessation of print publication and a transition to all-digital format at the end of 2012. The print edition then relaunched in March 2014 under different ownership.

Revenue declines prompted an August 2010 sale by owner The Washington Post Company to audio pioneer Sidney Harman—for a purchase price of one dollar and an assumption of the magazine's liabilities. Later that year, *Newsweek* merged with the news and opinion website The Daily Beast, forming The *Newsweek* Daily Beast Company. *Newsweek* was jointly owned by the estate of Harman and the diversified American media and Internet company IAC. In 2013, IBT Media announced it had acquired *Newsweek* from IAC; the acquisition included the *Newsweek* brand and its online publication, but did not include The Daily Beast. IBT Media rebranded itself as *Newsweek* Media Group in 2017, but returned to IBT Media in 2018 after making *Newsweek* independent.

---

* https://en.wikipedia.org/wiki/Newsweek

*Newsweek*는 1933년 Time 지의 외신 편집자인 Thomas J. C. Martyn이 창간했으며 20세기 내내 널리 배포된 시사주간지이다. *Newsweek*는 1961년 The Washington Post Company에 인수되어 2010년까지 운영되었으며, 2008년과 2012년 사이 재정적인 어려움으로 인해 인쇄 출판을 중단하고, 2012년 말 디지털 체제로 전환되었다. 2014년 3월 소유자가 바뀌면서 인쇄 출판이 다시 시작되었다.

Smart Vocabulary

notable: 주목할 만한; 저명한, 유명한
editor in chief: 편집장, 주필
cessation: 정지, 휴지, 중지
transition: 변이(變移), 추이
relaunch: 재출발시키다, 다시 시작하게 하다
decline: 쇠퇴, 감퇴
assumption 인수, 수락; 가정, 억측
liability: 책임, 의무; (pl.) 빚, 채무
estate: 재산
diversify: 다양화하다; (투자대상을) 분산시키다
acquisition: 취득, 획득; 습득
rebrand: (기업의) 이미지 변화를 꾀하다

40. New York Times *

The New York Times is an American newspaper based in New York City with worldwide influence and readership. Founded in 1851, the paper has won 127 Pulitzer Prizes, more than any other newspaper. The *Times* is ranked 18th in the world by circulation and 3rd in the U.S. Nicknamed "The Gray Lady," the *Times* has long been regarded within the industry as a national "newspaper of record." The paper's motto, "All the News That's Fit to Print", appears in the upper left-hand corner of the front page.

The paper is owned by The New York Times Company, which is publicly traded and is controlled by the Sulzberger family through a dual-class share structure. It has been owned by the family since 1896; A.G. Sulzberger, the paper's publisher, and his father, Arthur Ochs Sulzberger Jr., the company's chairman, are the fourth and fifth generation of the family to head the paper.

Since the mid-1970s, *The New York Times* has greatly expanded its layout and organization, adding special weekly sections on various topics supplementing the regular news, editorials, sports, and features. Since 2008, the *Times* has been organized into the following sections: News, Editorials/Opinions-Columns/Op-Ed, New York (metropolitan), Business, Sports of The Times, Arts, Science, Styles, Home, Travel, and other features.

---

* https://en.wikipedia.org/wiki/The_New_York_Times

The New York Times 는 1851년에 설립되었으며 다른 어떤 신문보다도 전 세계적인 영향력과 독자들을 갖고 있다. *New York Times* 는 127개의 Pulitzer Prize를 받았고, 발행 부수로는 세계에서 18위, 미국에서 3위를 차지했으며 "The Gray Lady"라는 별명을 갖고 있다. 또한 이 신문은 오랫동안 국가적인 "newspaper of record"으로 여겨져 왔으며, 모토인 "All the News That's Fit to Print"는 1면 왼쪽 상단에 있다.

Smart Vocabulary

readership: (특정 신문·잡지 등의) 독자 수
circulation: 발행 부수; (도서의) 대출 부수
head: …을 지휘하다, 이끌다
supplement: 보충하다; 추가하다
editorial: (신문의) 사설, 논설
feature: (신문·잡지 따위의) 특집기사; 특집란

41. Washington Post *

The Washington Post (sometimes abbreviated to WaPo) is a major American daily newspaper published in Washington, D.C. Daily broadsheet editions are printed for the District of Columbia, Maryland, and Virginia.

The newspaper has won 47 Pulitzer Prizes. This includes six separate Pulitzers awarded in 2008, second only to *The New York Times*'s seven awards in 2002 for the highest number ever awarded to a single newspaper in one year. Post journalists have also received 18 Nieman Fellowships and 368 White House News Photographers Association awards. In the early 1970s, in the best-known episode in the newspaper's history, reporters Bob Woodward and Carl Bernstein led the American press's investigation into what became known as the Watergate scandal. Their reporting in *The Washington Post* greatly contributed to the resignation of President Richard Nixon. In years since, the Post's investigations have led to increased review of the Walter Reed Army Medical Center.

In October 2013, the paper's longtime controlling family, the Graham family, sold the newspaper to Nash Holdings, a holding company established by Jeff Bezos, for $250 million in cash.

---

* https://en.wikipedia.org/wiki/The_Washington_Post

The Washington Post 는 1877년 12월 6일 Stilson Hutchins이 창간한 이래 여러 차례 매각되고, 1933년에 Eugene Meyer가 경영권을 인수한 후 비로서 미국의 유력지가 된다. 1970년대 초 Bob Woodward와 Carl Bernstein 기자가 Watergate scandal에 대한 보도를 이끌었으며, 결국 Richard Nixon 대통령의 사임을 이끌어 냈다는 사실은 *The Washington Post* 역사상 가장 잘 알려진 일화이다.

Smart Vocabulary

abbreviate: 생략(단축, 요약)하다
broadsheet: 보통 사이즈의 신문(연예·오락 관련 기사를 주로 다루는 타블로이드 판 신문에 비해 진지한 신문으로 여겨짐)
holding company: 지주회사
contribute: 기여(공헌)하다
resignation: 사직, 사임

42. Citibank *

Citibank (stylized as citibank) is the consumer division of financial services multinational Citigroup. Citibank was founded in 1812 as the City Bank of New York, and later became First National City Bank of New York. The bank has 2,649 branches in 19 countries, including 723 branches in the United States and 1,494 branches in Mexico operated by its subsidiary Banamex. The U.S. branches are concentrated in six metropolitan areas: New York City, Chicago, Los Angeles, San Francisco, Washington, D.C., and Miami. In 2016, the United States accounted for 70% of revenue and Mexico accounted for 13% of revenue. Aside from the U.S. and Mexico, most of the company's branches are in Poland, Russia, India and the United Arab Emirates.

As a result of the financial crisis of 2007–2008 and huge losses in the value of its subprime mortgage assets, Citigroup, the parent of Citibank, received a bailout in the form of an investment from the U.S. Treasury. On November 23, 2008, in addition to an initial investment of $25 billion, a further $20 billion was invested in the company along with guarantees for risky assets of $306 billion. The guarantees were issued at a time markets were not confident Citi had enough liquidity to cover losses from those investments. Eventually the Citi shares the Treasury took over in return for the guarantees it issued were booked as net profit for the treasury as Citi had enough liquidity and guarantees did not have to be used. By 2010, Citibank had repaid the loans from the Treasury in full, including interest, resulting in a net profit for the U.S. federal government.

---

* https://en.wikipedia.org/wiki/Citibank

Citibank는 1812년 6월 16일 City Bank of New York으로 설립되었고, 이에 First National City Bank of New York이 되었다. Citibank는 미국에 723개 지점이 있고 자회사인 Banamex가 운영하는 멕시코의 1,494개 지점 등, 19개국에 2,649개의 지점을 보유하고 있다. 미국 지점은 6개의 대도시 New York City, Chicago, Los Angeles, San Francisco, Washington, D.C., and Miami에 집중되어 있다.

Smart Vocabulary

stylize: 인습적으로 하다; [미술] (도안 등을) 일정한 양식에 맞추다
subsidiary: 자회사
revenue: 소득, 수입
subprime: 비우량의
mortgage: 대출(금), 융자(금)
asset: 자산, 재산
bailout: 긴급 원조(구제)
Treasury: (미국의) 재무부
guarantee: 보증(security); 담보(물)
liquidity: 유동성
net profit: 순(이)익

43. Black Friday *

Black Friday is an informal name for the Friday following Thanksgiving Day in the United States, which is celebrated on the fourth Thursday of November. The day after Thanksgiving has been regarded as the beginning of the United States Christmas shopping season since 1952, although the term "Black Friday" did not become widely used until more recent decades.

Many stores offer highly promoted sales on Black Friday and open very early, such as at midnight, or may even start their sales at some time on Thanksgiving. Black Friday is not an official holiday, but California and some other states observe "The Day After Thanksgiving" as a holiday for state government employees, sometimes in lieu of another federal holiday, such as Columbus Day. Many non-retail employees and schools have both Thanksgiving and the following Friday off, which, along with the following regular weekend, makes it a four-day weekend, thereby increasing the number of potential shoppers.

Black Friday has routinely been the busiest shopping day of the year in the United States since 2005, although news reports, which at that time were inaccurate, have described it as the busiest shopping day of the year for a much longer period of time. Similar stories resurface year upon year at this time, portraying hysteria and shortage of stock, creating a state of positive feedback.

---

* https://en.wikipedia.org/wiki/Black_Friday_(shopping)

Black Friday는 11월의 네 번째 목요일인 Thanksgiving Day의 다음날 금요일의 비공식적인 이름이다. Thanksgiving Day 다음 날은 1952년 이후 미국 크리스마스 쇼핑 시즌의 시작으로 간주되어 왔다. Black Friday는 공식적인 공휴일이 아니지만, California와 다른 주에서는 "Thanksgiving 다음 날"을 때때로 Columbus Day와 같은 연방 공휴일 대신에 주 정부 직원들을 위한 휴일로 지키고 있다.

Smart Vocabulary

observe; (법률 · 풍습 · 규정 · 시간 따위를) 지키다, 준수하다
in lieu of: …의 대신으로(instead of)
potential: 잠재적인; 가능한
resurface: …의 표지를 바꾸다; 다시 떠오르다

44. Halloween[*]

Halloween or Hallowe'en (a contraction of Hallows' Even or Hallows' Evening), also known as Allhalloween, All Hallows' Eve, or All Saints' Eve, is a celebration observed in several countries on 31 October, the eve of the Western Christian feast of All Hallows' Day. It begins the three-day observance of Allhallowtide, the time in the liturgical year dedicated to remembering the dead, including saints (hallows), martyrs, and all the faithful departed.

It is widely believed that many Halloween traditions originated from ancient Celtic harvest festivals, particularly the Gaelic festival Samhain; that such festivals may have had pagan roots; and that Samhain itself was Christianized as Halloween by the early Church. Some believe, however, that Halloween began solely as a Christian holiday, separate from ancient festivals like Samhain.

---

[*] https://en.wikipedia.org/wiki/Halloween

Halloween은 서양 기독교의 축제인 All Hallows' Day(모든 성인 대축일)의 전야인 10월 31일에 행해지는 축제이다. Halloween은 성인(할로윈), 순교자, 모든 죽은 신자들을 포함해서 고인을 기억하기 위해 전례에 정한 시기인 Allhallowtide 3일 간의 의식을 시작한다.

Smart Vocabulary

contraction: 단축; 수축
feast: 축제(일)《주로 종교상의》
liturgical: 전례(典禮)의; 성찬식의
departed: 고인(故人); 죽은
pagan: 이교도(異敎徒)

45. Starbucks *

Starbucks Corporation is an American coffee company and coffeehouse chain. Starbucks was founded in Seattle, Washington in 1971. As of early 2019, the company operates over 30,000 locations worldwide.

Starbucks has been described as the main representative of "second wave coffee," a retrospectively termed movement that popularized artisanal coffee, particularly darkly roasted coffee. Since the 2000s, third wave coffee makers have targeted quality-minded coffee drinkers with hand-made coffee based on lighter roasts, while Starbucks nowadays uses automated espresso machines for efficiency and safety reasons.

Starbucks locations serve hot and cold drinks, whole-bean coffee, microground instant coffee known as VIA, espresso, caffe latte, full- and loose-leaf teas including Teavana tea products, Evolution Fresh juices, Frappuccino beverages, La Boulange pastries, and snacks including items such as chips and crackers; some offerings (including their annual fall launch of the Pumpkin Spice Latte) are seasonal or specific to the locality of the store. Many stores sell pre-packaged food items, hot and cold sandwiches, and drinkware including mugs and tumblers; select "Starbucks Evenings" locations offer beer, wine, and appetizers. Starbucks-brand coffee, ice cream, and bottled cold coffee drinks are also sold at grocery stores.

---

* https://en.wikipedia.org/wiki/Starbucks

Starbucks는 1971년 Gordon Bowker, Gerald Jerry Baldwin, Zev Siegl이 Washington 주 Seattle에 설립한 커피 프랜차이즈 브랜드로서, 2019년 현재 전 세계에서 30,000개 이상의 매장을 운영하고 있다. Starbucks라는 이름은 미국의 소설가 Herman Melville의 대표적인 소설인 *Moby-Dick*에 등장하는 일등 항해사 Starbuck의 이름에서 유래했다.

Smart Vocabulary

corporation: 유한 회사, 주식회사; 법인, 협회
describe: 묘사하다; 설명하다
representative: 대표자, 대리인; 표본; 전형
retrospective: 회고의; 과거로 거슬러 올라가는
term: 이름짓다, 칭하다, 부르다
artisan: 솜씨 좋은 직공, 기술공, 숙련공
roast: (콩·커피 열매 따위를) 볶다
efficiency: 효율, 능률
locality: 위치, 장소

46. McDonald's *

McDonald's Corporation is an American fast food company, founded in 1940 as a restaurant operated by Richard and Maurice McDonald, in San Bernardino, California, United States. They rechristened their business as a hamburger stand, and later turned the company into a franchise, with the Golden Arches logo being introduced in 1953 at a location in Phoenix, Arizona. In 1955, Ray Kroc, a businessman, joined the company as a franchise agent and proceeded to purchase the chain from the McDonald brothers. McDonald's had its original headquarters in Oak Brook, Illinois, but moved its global headquarters to Chicago in early 2018.

McDonald's is the world's largest restaurant chain by revenue, serving over 69 million customers daily in over 100 countries across 37,855 outlets as of 2018. Although McDonald's is best known for its hamburgers, cheeseburgers and french fries, they also feature chicken products, breakfast items, soft drinks, milkshakes, wraps, and desserts. In response to changing consumer tastes and a negative backlash because of the unhealthiness of their food, the company has added to its menu salads, fish, smoothies, and fruit. The McDonald's Corporation revenues come from the rent, royalties, and fees paid by the franchisees, as well as sales in company-operated restaurants. According to two reports published in 2018, McDonald's is the world's second-largest private employer with 1.7 million employees (behind Walmart with 2.3 million employees).

---

* https://en.wikipedia.org/wiki/McDonald%27s

McDonald's는 1948년 Richard James McDonald와 Maurice James McDonald 형제가 California 주 San Bernardino에서 운영한 레스토랑이다. 그들은 1953년 Arizona 주 Phoenix에서 Golden Arches 로고를 도입하면서 햄버거 가게로 만들고, 1955년 Ray Kroc은 McDonald 형제로부터 프렌차이즈 운영권을 구입하게 된다. McDonald's의 본사는 원래 Illinois 주 Oak Brook에 있었으나, 2018년 초 Chicago로 이전한다.

Smart Vocabulary

rechristen: (세례하여) 다시 명명하다, 새로 이름을 붙이다
proceed: (앞으로) 나아가다; (일 따위가) 진행되다
revenue: 소득, 수입
backlash: 반발, 반격

47. KFC *

KFC, also known as Kentucky Fried Chicken, is an American fast food restaurant chain headquartered in Louisville, Kentucky, that specializes in fried chicken. It is the world's second-largest restaurant chain (as measured by sales) after McDonald's, with 22,621 locations globally in 136 countries as of December 2018. The chain is a subsidiary of Yum! Brands, a restaurant company that also owns the Pizza Hut, Taco Bell and WingStreet chains.

KFC was founded by Colonel Harland Sanders, an entrepreneur who began selling fried chicken from his roadside restaurant in Corbin, Kentucky, during the Great Depression. Sanders identified the potential of the restaurant franchising concept, and the first "Kentucky Fried Chicken" franchise opened in Utah in 1952. KFC popularized chicken in the fast food industry, diversifying the market by challenging the established dominance of the hamburger. By branding himself as "Colonel Sanders", Harland became a prominent figure of American cultural history, and his image remains widely used in KFC advertising to this day. However, the company's rapid expansion overwhelmed the aging Sanders, and he sold it to a group of investors led by John Y. Brown Jr. and Jack C. Massey in 1964.

---

* https://en.wikipedia.org/wiki/KFC

Kentucky Fried Chicken는 대공황 시기에 Colonel Harland Sanders가 Kentucky 주Corbin의 길가 레스토랑에서 치킨을 팔기 시작한 패스트푸드 체인점이다. 1952년 Sanders는 Utah 주 Salt Lake City에서 첫 번째 점포를 열었으며 Kentucky 주 Louisville에 본사가 있다. 현재 KFC는 McDonald's에 이어 세계에서 두 번째로 큰 레스토랑 체인으로서, Pizza Hut, Taco Bell, WingStreet를 소유한 YUM! Brands, Inc의 자회사이다.

Smart Vocabulary

subsidiary: 자회사
entrepreneur: 실업가, 기업가
identify: 확인하다; 인지(판정)하다; (…와) 동일시하다
diversify: 다양화하다; (투자대상을) 분산시키다
dominance: 우세, 우월; 지배
overwhelm: 압도하다

48. Burger King *

Burger King (BK) is an American multinational chain of hamburger fast food restaurants. Headquartered in the unincorporated area of Miami-Dade County, Florida, the company was founded in 1953 as Insta-Burger King, a Jacksonville, Florida–based restaurant chain. After Insta-Burger King ran into financial difficulties in 1954, its two Miami-based franchisees David Edgerton and James McLamore purchased the company and renamed it "Burger King". Over the next half-century, the company changed hands four times, with its third set of owners, a partnership of TPG Capital, Bain Capital, and Goldman Sachs Capital Partners, taking it public in 2002. In late-2010, 3G Capital of Brazil acquired a majority stake in the company, in a deal valued at US$3.26 billion. The new owners promptly initiated a restructuring of the company to reverse its fortunes. 3G, along with partner Berkshire Hathaway, eventually merged the company with the Canadian-based doughnut chain Tim Hortons, under the auspices of a new Canadian-based parent company named Restaurant Brands International.

---

* https://en.wikipedia.org/wiki/Burger_King

Burger King은 1953년 Insta-Burger King이라는 이름으로 설립된 되었고 미국의 다국적 패스트푸드 회사로서 Florida 주에 본사가 있다. 1954년 Insta-Burger King가 재정난에 빠지자 James Mclamore와 David Edgerton가 이 회사를 인수하여 Burger King으로 이름을 바꾸며, 이후 네 번에 걸쳐 소유주가 바뀌게 된다. 2018년 12월 31일 현재, Burger King은 100여개 국가에서 17,796개의 지점이 있으며, 그 중 거의 절반이 미국에 있다.

Smart Vocabulary

unincorporated: 합병되지 않은; 법인 조직이 아닌
run into: (~에) 빠지다
financial difficulties: 재정난
change hands: 임자가 바뀌다
stake: 소액의 (목)돈; 주(株)의 보유분
reverse: 거꾸로 하다, 반대로 하다; 뒤집다
fortune: 운명, 숙명, 운수; (종종 pl.) 인생의 부침, 성쇠
merge: 합병하다
auspice: (pl.) 후원, 찬조, 보호.

49. Popeyes [*]

Popeyes is an American multinational chain of fried chicken fast food restaurants founded in 1972 in New Orleans, Louisiana and headquartered in Miami, Florida. Since 2008, its full brand name is Popeyes Louisiana Kitchen, Inc., and it was formerly named Popeyes Chicken & Biscuits and Popeyes Famous Fried Chicken & Biscuits. It is currently a subsidiary of Toronto-based Restaurant Brands International.

According to a company press release dated June 29, 2007, Popeyes is the second-largest "quick-service chicken restaurant group, measured by number of units", after KFC. Popeyes has 3,102 restaurants, which are located in more than 40 states and the District of Columbia, Puerto Rico, and 30 countries worldwide. About thirty locations are company-owned, the rest franchised.

---

[*] https://en.wikipedia.org/wiki/Popeyes

Popeyes는 1972년 6월 12일 Louisiana 주 New Orleans에 설립된 미국의 다국적 치킨 패스트푸드 체인점으로서 본사는 Florida주의 Miami에 있다. 오너인 Al Copeland는 "Chicken on the Run"라는 이름으로 처음 문을 열고 Kentucky Fried Chicken과 경쟁하기를 원했지만, 그의 레스토랑은 몇 달 만에 실패했다. 사일 후 Copeland가 그것을 Popeyes Mighty Good Chicken라고 이름을 바꾸고, 1975년 Popeyes Famous Fried Chicken로 개명한 후, Louisiana 주에서부터 레스토랑을 프랜차이즈로 바꾸기 시작했다. 2008년 이래로, Popeyes의 브랜드명은 Popeyes Louisiana Kitchen, Inc.이며, 현재 Toronto에 본사가 있는 Restaurant Brands International의 자회사이다.

Smart Vocabulary

subsidiary: 자회사
press release: 보도 자료

50. Subway [*]

Subway is an American privately-held restaurant franchise that primarily sells submarine sandwiches (subs) and salads. It is one of the fastest-growing franchises in the world and, as of October 2019, had 41,512 locations in more than 100 countries. More than half its locations (23,928 or 57.6%) are in the United States. It also is the largest single-brand restaurant chain, and the largest restaurant operator, in the world.

As of 2017, the Subway Group of companies was organized as follows:

1. Subway IP Inc. is the owner of the intellectual property for the restaurant system.
2. Franchise World Headquarters, LLC leads franchising operations. FWH Technologies, LLC owns and licenses Subway's point of sale software.
3. Franchisors include Doctor's Associates Inc. in the U.S.; Subway International B.V.; Subway Franchise Systems of Canada, Ltd.; etc.
4. Advertising affiliates include Subway Franchisee Advertising Fund Trust, Ltd.; Subway Franchisee Advertising Fund Trust, B.V.; Subway Franchisee Canadian Advertising Trust; etc.

Subway's core product is the submarine sandwich (or "sub"). In addition to these, the chain also sells wraps, salad, paninis, and baked goods (including cookies, doughnuts, and muffins).

Subway's best-selling sandwich, the B.M.T. (short for "Biggest, Meatiest, Tastiest"), contains pepperoni, salami, and ham. The name originally stood for Brooklyn Manhattan Transit.

Subway also sells breakfast sandwiches, English muffins, and flatbread. In 2006, "personal pizzas" debuted in some US markets. These are made to order (like the subs) and heated for 85 seconds. Breakfast and pizza items are only available in some stores. In November 2009, Subway signed a deal to serve exclusively Seattle's Best Coffee coffee as part of its breakfast menu in the US.

---

[*] https://en.wikipedia.org/wiki/Subway

Subway는 1965년 Fred DeLuca는 친구인 Peter Buck에게 1,000달러를 빌려서 Connecticut 주 Bridgeport에서 "Pete's Super Submarines"를 시작하고, 그 다음 해 그들은 Doctor's Associates Inc.를 창업하였다. 1968년, 샌드위치 가게는 "Subway"로 이름을 변경했고, 본사는 Connecticut주 Milford에 있다. Subway에서 가장 많이 팔리는 샌드위치인 B.M.T. ("Biggest, Meatiest, Tastiest")는 페퍼로니와 살라미, 햄이 들어있으며, B.M.T.라는 이름은 원래 Brooklyn-Manhattan Transit 시스템에서 비롯된 것이다.

Smart Vocabulary

submarine sandwich: 긴 롤빵에 냉육 · 치즈 · 야채를 끼운 큰 샌드위치
intellectual property: 지적 재산; 지적 재산권
as of: 현재
affiliate: 계열(자매) 회사

51. Taco Bell [*]

Taco Bell is an American chain of fast food restaurants based in Irvine, California and a subsidiary of Yum! Brands, Inc. The restaurants serve a variety of Mexican inspired foods that include tacos, burritos, quesadillas, and nachos.

History

Taco Bell was founded by Glen Bell, who first opened a hot dog stand called Bell's Drive-In in San Bernardino, California in 1962 in Downey, California. in 1967, the 100th restaurant opened at 400 South Brookhurst in Anaheim. Original Taco Bell's featured walk-up windows only, with no indoor seating or drive-thru service. In 1968, its first franchise location east of the Mississippi River opened in Springfield, Ohio. In 1970, Taco Bell went public with 325 restaurants.

---

* https://en.wikipedia.org/wiki/Taco_Bell

Taco Bell은 California 주 Irvine에 본사가 있는 패스트푸드 레스토랑 체인이며, Yum! Brands, Inc.의 자회사이다. Taco Bell은 1948년 Glen Bell이 California주 San Bernardino에서 Bell's Drive-In이라는 핫도그 가판대로 처음 시작했으며, 1962년 California 주 Downey에 Taco Bell을 열었다. taco는 멕시코의 대중적 음식으로서 토르티야에 고기, 해물, 채소 등 다양한 재료를 싸서 먹는 샌드위치이다.

Smart Vocabulary

subsidiary: 자회사
inspire: (어떤 사상·감정 등을) …에게 불어넣다
walk-up: 엘리베이터가 없는 건물
go public: (회사가) 주식을 공개하다

52. Pizza Hut

Pizza Hut is an American restaurant chain and international franchise which was founded in 1958 in Wichita, Kansas by Dan and Frank Carney. The company is known for its Italian American cuisine menu, including pizza and pasta, as well as side dishes and desserts. Pizza Hut has 18,431 restaurants worldwide as of December 31, 2018, making it the world's largest pizza chain in terms of locations. It is a subsidiary of Yum! Brands, Inc., one of the world's largest restaurant companies.

History

Pizza Hut was founded in June 1958 by two Wichita State University students, brothers Dan and Frank Carney, as a single location in Wichita, Kansas. Six months later they opened a second outlet and within a year they had six Pizza Hut restaurants. The brothers began franchising in 1959. The iconic Pizza Hut building style was designed in 1963 by Chicago architect George Lindstrom and was implemented in 1969. PepsiCo acquired Pizza Hut in November 1977. 20 years later, Pizza Hut (alongside Taco Bell and Kentucky Fried Chicken) were spun off by PepsiCo on May 30, 1997, and all three restaurant chains became part of a new company named Tricon Global Restrauants, Inc. The company assumed the name of Yum! Brands on May 22, 2002.

Pizza Hut은 1958년 Kansas주 Wichita에서 Dan Carney와 Frank Carney 형제가 설립한 레스토랑 체인이며 국제적인 프랜차이즈 브랜드이다. 대학생이었던 형제는 어머니에게서 돈을 빌려 당시 미국에서 생소했던 Pizza를 아이템으로 정하여 창업하게 되었고, 일 년 뒤 1959년 Topeka에 첫 번째 프랜차이즈 점을 열었다. 1977년 PepsiCo Inc.는 KFC, Taco Bell과 함께 Pizza Hut을 인수했고, 2002년 레스토랑 브랜드를 Yam! Brands로 분리시켰다.

Smart Vocabulary

cuisine: 요리 솜씨, 요리(법)
side dish: (주(主)요리에) 곁들여 내는 요리; 그 접시
as of: 현재
in terms of: ~에 의하여; ~에 관하여; ~의 점에서 (보아)
subsidiary: 자회사
implement: 이행(실행)하다

53. Domino's Pizza [*]

Domino's Pizza, Inc., branded as Domino's, is an American multinational pizza restaurant chain founded in 1960. The corporation is headquartered at the Domino's Farms Office Park in Ann Arbor, Michigan, and incorporated in Delaware. In February 2018, the chain became the largest pizza seller worldwide in terms of sales.

History

In 1960, Tom Monaghan and his brother, James, took over the operation of DomiNick's, an existing location of a small pizza restaurant chain that had been owned by Dominick DiVarti, at 507 Cross Street (now 301 West Cross Street) in Ypsilanti, Michigan, near Eastern Michigan University. The deal was secured by a $500 down payment, and the brothers borrowed $900 to pay for the store. The brothers planned to split the work hours evenly, but James did not want to quit his job as a full-time postman to keep up with the demands of the new business. Within eight months, James traded his half of the business to Tom for the Volkswagen Beetle they used for pizza deliveries.

By 1965, Tom Monaghan had purchased two additional pizzerias; he now had a total of three locations in the same county. Monaghan wanted the stores to share the same branding, but the original owner forbade him from using the DomiNick's name. One day, an employee, Jim Kennedy, returned from a pizza delivery and suggested the name "Domino's". Monaghan immediately loved the idea and officially renamed the business Domino's Pizza, Inc. in 1965.

---

[*] https://en.wikipedia.org/wiki/Domino%27s_Pizza

> Domino's Pizza는 1960년 Michigan주 Ypsilanti에서 형제인 Tom Monaghan과 James가 작은 피자 레스토랑 체인점인 DomiNick's를 인수하며 시작한 피자 배달 전문 브랜드로서 1965년 직원의 제안을 받아들여 Domino's Pizza로 개명했다.

Smart Vocabulary

corporation: 법인; 주식회사
incorporate: 법인(조직)으로 만들다; 주식회사로 하다
in terms of: ~에 의하여; ~에 관하여; ~의 점에서 (보아)
evenly: 공평하게
forbid: (…을) 금지하다, 허용치 않다

54. Coca-Cola *

The Coca-Cola Company is an American multinational corporation, and manufacturer, retailer, and marketer of alcoholic beverage concentrates and syrups. The company produces Coca-Cola, invented in 1886 by pharmacist John Stith Pemberton in Atlanta, Georgia. In 1889 the formula and brand were sold for $2,300 to Asa Griggs Candler, who incorporated The Coca-Cola Company in Atlanta in 1892. The Coca-Cola Company is the single largest plastic polluter in the world, producing over 3 million tonnes of plastic packaging each year including 110 billion plastic bottles.

The company—headquartered in Atlanta, Georgia, but incorporated in Delaware—has operated a franchised distribution system since 1889: the Company largely produces syrup concentrate, which is then sold to various bottlers throughout the world who hold exclusive territories. The company owns its anchor bottler in North America, Coca-Cola Refreshments. The company's stock is listed on the NYSE and is part of DJIA, the S&P 500 index, the Russell 1000 Index, and the Russell 1000 Growth Stock Index.

---

* https://en.wikipedia.org/wiki/The_Coca-Cola_Company

Coca-Cola는 1886년 Georgia주 Atlanta에서 약제사인 John Stith Pemberton이 Coca 나뭇잎, Cola의 열매, 시럽 등으로 제조하여 판매했다. 1889년 Pemberton은 약제사인 Asa Griggs Candler에게 2300달러를 받고 제조법과 판매권을 팔았고, 1892년 Candler는 Atlanta에 The Coca-Cola Company를 세웠다.

Smart Vocabulary

multinational corporation: 다국적 기업
manufacturer: 제조(업)자
retailer: 소매상인
alcoholic beverage: 알코올 음료
concentrate: 농축물(액)
pharmacist: 약사(=pharmaceutis)
formula: 제조법; (약 따위의) 처방(전); (요리의) 조리법
incorporate: 법인(조직)으로 만들다; 주식회사로 하다
polluter: 오염자(원(源))
tonn: (선박의) 용적 톤수(=tonnage)
distribution: (상품의) 판매, 유통
exclusive: 독점적인; 배타적인
territory: 영토; 영역, 분야; (외판원 따위의) 담당구역 세력권
anchor: 주요거점
bottler: 탄산음료 제조업자
stock: 주식, 증권
NYSE: 뉴욕 증권 거래소 (New York Stock Exchange)
index: 지표; 지수
DJIA: 다우존스 공업주 평균주가 (Dow-Jones Industrial Average)
Growth Stock: 성장주

55. Pepsi Cola *

Pepsi is a carbonated soft drink manufactured by PepsiCo. Originally created and developed in by Caleb Bradham and introduced as Brad's Drink, it was renamed as Pepsi-Cola in 1898, and then shortened to Pepsi in 1961.

Rivalry with Coca-Cola

According to Consumer Reports, in the 1970s, the rivalry continued to heat up the market. Pepsi conducted blind taste tests in stores, in what was called the "Pepsi Challenge". These tests suggested that more consumers preferred the taste of Pepsi to Coca-Cola. The sales of Pepsi started to climb, and Pepsi kicked off the "Challenge" across the nation. This became known as the "Cola Wars".

---

* https://en.wikipedia.org/wiki/Pepsi

Pepsi는 1893년 Caleb Bradham가 North Carolina주 New Bern에 있는 자신의 약국에서 Brad's drink라는 이름으로 처음 만들어 판매한 탄산음료이다. 그 후 1898년 8월 28일 Brad's drink는 "소화"(digestion)라는 의미를 갖고 있는 그리스어 "πέψη"와 똑같이 발음되는 Pepsi와 콜라 열매(kola nut)에서 "cola"를 따서 Pepsi-Cola로 이름을 바꾸고, 1961년 Pepsi가 된다.

Smart Vocabulary

carbonated drink: 탄산음료
soft drink: 청량음료
manufacture: 제조 (제작, 생산)하다《특히 대규모로》
rivalry: 경쟁
heat up: 격해지다; (행위 따위가) 한층 더 열기를 띠다
blind test: 피(被)시험자가 내용을 모르고 하는 화학상의 검사; 예비지식이나 선입감 없이 하 는 테스트
kick off: 시작하다

56. Baskin Robbins *

Baskin Robbins is an American chain of ice cream and cake specialty shop restaurants. Its parent company is Dunkin' Brands. Based in Canton, Massachusetts, Baskin-Robbins was founded in 1945 by Burt Baskin and Irv Robbins in Glendale, California. It claims to be the world's largest chain of ice cream specialty stores, with more than 8,000 locations, including nearly 2,500 shops in the United States and over 5,000 in other countries. Baskin-Robbins sells ice cream in nearly 50 countries.

The company is known for its "31 flavors" slogan, with the idea that a customer could have a different flavor every day of any month. The slogan came from the Carson-Roberts advertising agency (which later merged into Ogilvy & Mather) in 1953. Baskin and Robbins believed that people should be able to sample flavors for free until they found one they wanted to buy.

---

* https://en.wikipedia.org/wiki/Baskin-Robbins

Baskin Robbins는 1945년 California 주 Glendale에서 Burt Baskin과 Irv Robbins가 설립한 아이스크림과 케이크 전문 프랜차이즈로서 모기업은 Dunkin' Brands이다. Baskin Robbins는 1945년 이래로 1,300개 이상의 맛을 소개해 왔으며, 미국에 거의 2,500개의 매장과 전 세계적으로 5,000개 이상의 매장을 두고 있다. 본사는 2004년 Massachusetts 주 Randolph에서 Canton으로 옮겼다.

Smart Vocabulary

parent company: 모(母)회사
sample: 시식(시음)하다

57. Amazon *

Amazon.com, Inc. is an American multinational technology company based in Seattle that focuses on e-commerce, cloud computing, digital streaming, and artificial intelligence. It is considered one of the Big Four tech companies, along with Google, Apple, and Facebook.

Amazon is known for its disruption of well-established industries through technological innovation and mass scale. It is the world's largest online marketplace, AI assistant provider, and cloud computing platform as measured by revenue and market capitalization. Amazon is the largest Internet company by revenue in the world. It is the second largest private employer in the United States and one of the world's most valuable companies.

Amazon was founded by Jeff Bezos in Bellevue, Washington, in July 1994. The company initially started as an online marketplace for books but later expanded to sell electronics, software, video games, apparel, furniture, food, toys, and jewelry. In 2015, Amazon surpassed Walmart as the most valuable retailer in the United States by market capitalization. In 2017, Amazon acquired Whole Foods Market for US$13.4 billion, which vastly increased Amazon's presence as a brick-and-mortar retailer. In 2018, Bezos announced that its two-day delivery service, Amazon Prime, had surpassed 100 million subscribers worldwide.

---

* https://en.wikipedia.org/wiki/Amazon_(company)

Amazon.com, Inc.는 1994년 7월 Washington 주 Bellevue에서 Jeff Bezos가 설립했으며, Seattle에 본사가 있는 다국적 기술 회사로서 Google, Apple, Facebook과 함께 Big Four 중의 하나로 꼽힌다. Amazon은 처음에는 책을 판매하는 온라인 시장으로 시작했지만, 후에 전자 제품, 소프트웨어, 비디오 게임, 옷, 가구, 음식, 장난감, 보석 등을 판매하게 된다. Amazon은 2015년 시가 총액으로 Walmart를 뛰어넘어 1위에 올랐으며, 2017년, 134억 달러에 Whole Foods Market을 인수했는데, 이것은 전통적인 유통업체로서 Amazon의 입지를 크게 높여 주었다. 2018년 Bezos는 이틀 내로 배송하는 서비스 Amazon Prime이 전 세계적으로 1억 명의 가입자를 넘어섰다고 발표했다.

Smart Vocabulary

artificial intelligence: 인공 지능
disruption: 붕괴, 와해; 혼란, 방해
innovation: 혁신, 일신, 쇄신
revenue: 소득, 수입
market capitalization: (유가 증권의) 시가 총액
apparel: 의복, 의상
surpass: ⋯보다 낫다, ⋯을 능가하다, ⋯을 넘다
brick-and-mortar: (인터넷을 사용하지 않는) 전통적인

58. Walmart *

Walmart Inc. is an American multinational retail corporation that operates a chain of hypermarkets, discount department stores, and grocery stores, headquartered in Bentonville, Arkansas. The company was founded by Sam Walton in 1962 and incorporated on October 31, 1969. It also owns and operates Sam's Club retail warehouses. As of October 31, 2019, Walmart has 11,438 stores and clubs in 27 countries, operating under 55 different names. The company operates under the name Walmart in the United States and Canada, as Walmart de México y Centroamérica in Mexico and Central America, as Asda in the United Kingdom, as the Seiyu Group in Japan, and as Best Price in India. It has wholly owned operations in Argentina, Chile, Canada, and South Africa. Since August 2018, Walmart only holds a minority stake in Walmart Brasil, which was renamed Grupo Big in August 2019, with 20 percent of the company's shares, and private equity firm Advent International holding 80 percent ownership of the company.

Walmart is the world's largest company by revenue, with US$514.405 billion, according to the list in 2019. It is also the largest private employer in the world with 2.2 million employees. It is a publicly traded family-owned business, as the company is controlled by the Walton family. Sam Walton's heirs own over 50 percent of Walmart through their holding company Walton Enterprises and through their individual holdings. Walmart was the largest U.S. grocery retailer in 2019, and 65 percent of Walmart's US$510.329 billion sales came from U.S. operations.

---

* https://en.wikipedia.org/wiki/Walmart

Walmart Inc.는 1962년 Sam Walton이 설립했고, 1969년 10월 31일 주식회사가 되었으며 Arkansas주 Bentonville에 본사가 있다. Walmart는 2019년 10월 31일 현재 27개국에서 11,438개의 매장과 Sam's Club을 보유하고 있으며, 미국과 캐나다에서는 Walmart, 멕시코와 중앙아메리카에서는 Walmart de México yCentroamericca, 영국에서는 Asda, 일본에서는 the Seiyu Group, 인도에서는 Best Price라는 이름으로 운영되는 등, 55개의 다른 이름으로 운영된다.

Walton's (1950 – 1969)
Wal-Mart, Inc. (1969 – 1970)
Wal-Mart Stores, Inc. (1970 – 2019)

Smart Vocabulary

hypermarket: (변두리의) 대형 슈퍼마켓
incorporate: 주식회사로 하다
warehouse: 창고, 저장소; 《英》도매상점, 큰 가게
As of: 현재
stake: 주(株)의 보유분
equity: (주식회사의) 지분; 주주 소유권; (pl.) 보통주
revenue: 소득, 수익
heir: 상속인, 법정 상속인
holding company: (타사 지배를 위한) 지주회사

59. Sam's Club *

Sam's West, Inc. (doing business as Sam's Club) is an American chain of membership-only retail warehouse clubs owned and operated by Walmart Inc., founded in 1983 and named after Walmart founder Sam Walton. As of January 31, 2019, Sam's Club ranks second in sales volume among warehouse clubs with $57.839 billion in sales (in fiscal year 2019) behind rival Costco Wholesale.

Its major competitors are Costco Wholesale and BJ's Wholesale Club.

As of January 31, 2020, Sam's Club operates 599 membership warehouse clubs in the United States in 44 states, Puerto Rico and the U.S Virgin Islands. Alaska (all three locations in that state closed in 2018 as part of a plan to close 63 clubs), Massachusetts (its last remaining location in that state, located in Worcester, closed in 2018 as part of a plan to close 63 clubs), Oregon, Rhode Island (the state's only location, in Warwick, closed in 2016 as part of a plan to close 269 stores globally, including four U.S. clubs), Vermont, and Washington (all three locations in that state closed in 2018 as part of a plan to close 63 clubs) are the only states where Sam's Club does not operate, as is the case for the District of Columbia. Walmart International also operates Sam's Club stores in Mexico and China. It has 163 locations in Mexico, and 26 in China. Grupo Big, formerly Walmart Brazil, which was de-consolidated from Walmart in August 2018, also operates Sam's Clubs in Brazil. Locations generally range in size from 34,000–168,000 sq ft (3,200–15,600 m2), with an average club size of approximately 134,000 sq ft (12,400 m2).

---

* https://en.wikipedia.org/wiki/Sam%27s_Club

Sam's West, Inc.는 1983년 4월 Walmart를 만든 Sam Walton의 이름을 따 Sam's Club으로 운영하는 회원제 창고형 할인매장이다. Sam's Club은 본사가 Arkansas 주 Bentonville에 있으며, 2019년 1월 31일 매출액 기준으로 창고형 매장 가운데 경쟁업체인 Costco Wholesale에 이어 세계에서 두 번째이다.

Smart Vocabulary

volume: 용적, 부피, 체적, 크기
fiscal year: 회계 연도
consolidate: 합병하다, 통합하다

60. Costco [*]

Costco Wholesale Corporation, doing business as Costco, is an American multinational corporation which operates a chain of membership-only warehouse clubs. As of 2015, Costco was the second largest retailer in the world after Walmart, and as of 2016, Costco was the world's largest retailer of choice and prime beef, organic foods, rotisserie chicken, and wine. As of 2019, Costco is ranked #14 on the Fortune 500 rankings of the largest United States corporations by total revenue.

Costco's worldwide headquarters are in Issaquah, Washington, a suburb east of Seattle; the company opened its first warehouse (the chain's term for its retail outlets) in Seattle 37 years ago in 1983. Through mergers, Costco's corporate history dates back to 1976, when its former competitor Price Club was founded in San Diego, California. As of December 31, 2019, Costco has a total of 785 warehouses: 546 in the United States and Puerto Rico, 100 in Canada, 39 in Mexico, 29 in the United Kingdom, 26 in Japan, 16 in South Korea, 13 in Taiwan, 11 in Australia, two in Spain, one in Iceland, one in France, and one in China. Costco is scheduled to open a warehouse in New Zealand in 2021.

---

[*] https://en.wikipedia.org/wiki/Costco

Costco Wholesale Corporation은 1983년 9월 Washington 주 Seattle에서 Jim Sinegal과 Jeffrey Brotman이 Costco Companies, Inc.라는 이름으로 첫 매장을 연 회원제 창고형 할인매장이다. 현재 Costco의 본사는 Seattle 근교인 Issaquah에 있으며, 2015년 현재 Walmart에 이어 전 세계에서 두 번째로 큰 소매업체이다.

Smart Vocabulary

rotisserie: (고기를) 꼬챙이에 꿰어 굽는 전기 기구
revenue: 소득, 수익
suburb: 교외, 근교
merger: (회사 등의) 합병

61. FedEx

FedEx Corporation is an American multinational delivery services company headquartered in Memphis, Tennessee. The name "FedEx" is a syllabic abbreviation of the name of the company's original air division, Federal Express (now FedEx Express), which was used from 1973 until 2000. The company is known for its overnight shipping service and pioneering a system that could track packages and provide real-time updates on package location, a feature that has now been implemented by most other carrier services.

logos

The FedEx logo is a wordmark designed in 1994 by Lindon Leader of Landor Associates, of San Francisco. It consists of Fed in purple and Ex in orange. The FedEx wordmark is notable for containing a subliminal right-pointing arrow in the negative space between the "E" and the "X", which was achieved by designing a proprietary font, based on Univers and Futura, to emphasize the arrow shape. Previously, the Ex was in a different color for each division and platinum for the overall corporation use. However, in August 2016, FedEx announced that all operating units will adopt the purple and orange color logo over the next five years (the same as the original FedEx logo, and later used by FedEx Express).

FedEx Corporation은 1971년 Frederick W. Smith가 Tennessee 주 Memphis에 세운 배송 업체이다. FedEx는 Federal Express를 줄인 말 1973년부터 2000년까지 사용했고, 현재는 FedEx Express이다. FedEx는 1973년 Memphis를 허브로 삼아 소화물을 운송하고, 24시간 안에 배송하는 서비스와 화물의 위치를 실시간으로 확인할 수 있는 화물추적 시스템을 도입했다.

Smart Vocabulary

syllabic: 음절의, 철자의
abbreviation: 생략
division: 구분, 부분; 부문
overnight: 하룻밤 사이의
shipping: 수송, 운송
implement: 이행(실행)하다
subliminal: 잠재의식의
proprietary: 독점의, 전매(특허)의
platinum: 【化】 백금
corporation: 주식 회사

62. U-Haul *

U-Haul is an American moving equipment and storage rental company, based in Phoenix, Arizona, that has been in operation since 1945. The company was founded by Leonard Shoen (L. S. "Sam" Shoen) in Ridgefield, Washington, who began it in the garage owned by his wife's family, and expanded it through franchising with gas stations.

History

In 1945 at the age of 29 Leonard Shoen co-founded U-Haul with his wife, Anna Mary Carty, in the town of Ridgefield, Washington, with an investment of $5,000. He began building rental trailers and splitting the fees for their use with gas station owners whom he franchised as agents. He developed one-way rentals and enlisted investors as partners in each trailer as methods of growth.

By 1955 there were more than 10,000 U-Haul trailers on the road, and the brand was nationally known. Distracted to some extent by growing his business, Shoen took time for multiple marriages and eventually had a total of 12 children, each of whom he made stockholders. Shoen transferred all but 2% of control to his children when two of them, Edward and Mark launched a successful takeover of the business in 1986. Family squabbling over the U-Haul empire turned to physical confrontations between some of his children at company meetings, even before the 1986 takeover. The takeover sparked a major family dispute that led to a $461 million judgment in favor of Leonard Shoen and others. In 1999, 83-year-old Leonard Shoen suffered fatal injuries when he crashed into a telephone pole near his Las Vegas, Nevada, home.

---

* https://en.wikipedia.org/wiki/U-Haul

FedEx Corporation은 1971년 Frederick W. Smith가 Tennessee 주 Memphis에 세운 배송 업체이다. FedEx는 Federal Express를 줄인 말 1973년부터 2000년까지 사용했고, 현재는 FedEx Express이다. FedEx는 1973년 Memphis를 허브로 삼아 소화물을 운송하고, 24시간 안에 배송하는 서비스와 화물의 위치를 실시간으로 확인할 수 있는 화물추적 시스템을 도입했다.

Smart Vocabulary

equipment: 장비, 설비
storage: 저장, 보관
in operation: 시행 중, 활동 중
split: 쪼개다(cleave); 분할하다
enlist: 협력을 얻다(구하다), 도움을 얻다
distract: (마음·주의 등을) 빗가게 하다, 흩뜨리다, (딴 데로) 돌리다(divert)
to some extent: ~ 어느 정도까지, 다소
stockholder: 주주(株主)
transfer: 옮기다, 이동(운반)하다; (재산·권리를) 양도하다
squabble: 시시한 일로 말다툼하다, 싸우다
in favor of: …에 찬성(지지)하여, …에 편을 들어

63. Greyhound *

Greyhound Lines, Inc., usually shortened to Greyhound, is an intercity bus common carrier serving over 3,800 destinations across North America. The company's first route began in Hibbing, Minnesota in 1914, and the company adopted the Greyhound name in 1929. Since October 2007, Greyhound has been a subsidiary of British transportation company FirstGroup, but continues to be based in Dallas, Texas, where it has been headquartered since 1987. Greyhound and its sister companies in FirstGroup America are the largest motorcoach operators in the United States and Canada

Services

Greyhound operates 123 routes serving over 2,700 destinations across the United States. Greyhound's scheduled services compete with the private automobile, low-cost airlines, Amtrak, and other intercity coach bus companies.

Greyhound Express is a low-cost express city-to-city service that makes either fewer stops or no stops compared to a traditional route. Fares start at $1 and seating is guaranteed since buses are not overbooked. Greyhound Express was designed to directly compete with low-cost carriers like Megabus and Chinatown bus lines.

Greyhound Connect is a connector service that operates shorter routes to take passengers from stops in smaller, rural cities to stations in larger, urban cities. Buses are either from Greyhound's existing fleet or smaller, mid-sized buses (that are not equipped with a lavatory). Currently the Greyhound Connect service is offered in Alabama, Arizona, Arkansas, Colorado, Maryland, Missouri, Montana, North Carolina, Utah, and Vermont. Some routes are operated using funds from the "Federal Formula Grant Program for Rural Areas" from the Federal Transit Administration.

---

* https://en.wikipedia.org/wiki/U-Haul

Greyhound Lines, Inc.는 1914년 Minnesota주 Hibbing에서 Carl Wickman이 설립했고 1929년 Greyhound라는 채택했으며, 2007년 이래 영국의 운송회사인 FirstGroup의 자회사가 된다. 1987년 이래 본사는 Texas주의 Dallas에 있으며, 북미 지역에서 3800개 이상의 도시를 운행한다.

Smart Vocabulary

intercity: (교통 등이) 도시 사이의(를 연결하는)
destination: 목적지, 행선지
adopt: 채용(채택)하다
subsidiary: 자회사
transportation: 운송, 수송; 《美》 교통(수송)기관
motorcoach: 버스(=motorbus)
lavatory: 세면소, 화장실

64. Amtrak *

The National Railroad Passenger Corporation, doing business as Amtrak, is a passenger railroad service that provides medium- and long-distance intercity service in the contiguous United States and to nine Canadian cities.

Founded in 1971 as a quasi-public corporation to operate many U.S. passenger rail services, it receives a combination of state and federal subsidies but is managed as a for-profit organization. Amtrak's headquarters is located one block west of Union Station in Washington, D.C.

Amtrak serves more than 500 destinations in 46 states and three Canadian provinces, operating more than 300 trains daily over 21,400 miles (34,000 km) of track. Amtrak owns approximately 623 miles of this track and operates an additional 132 miles of track. Some track sections allow trains to run as fast as 150 mph (240 km/h).

---

* https://en.wikipedia.org/wiki/Amtrak

전미 여객 철도공사(Amtrak)은 1971년에 설립된 준공영 기업으로서 주와 연방의 보조금을 받지만 영리 기관으로 운영된다. Amtrak의 본사는 Washington, D.C.에 있다.

Smart Vocabulary

contiguous: 접촉하는; 접근하는, 인접한
quasi-: 준(準), 유사(類似), 의사(擬似)
federal: 연방(정부)의
subsidy: (국가의 민간에 대한) 보조(장려)금
for-profit: (회사·사업이) 영리 목적의, 이익 추구의
union station: 합동역《둘 이상의 철도·버스 회사가 공동으로 사용하는 역》

65. American Airlines *

American Airlines, Inc. (AA) is a major American airline headquartered in Fort Worth, Texas, within the Dallas–Fort Worth metroplex. It is the world's largest airline when measured by fleet size, revenue, scheduled passengers carried, scheduled passenger-kilometers flown, and number of destinations served. American, together with its regional partners, operates an extensive international and domestic network with almost 6,800 flights per day to nearly 350 destinations in more than 50 countries. American Airlines is a founding member of the Oneworld alliance, the third largest airline alliance in the world. Regional service is operated by independent and subsidiary carriers under the brand name American Eagle.

American Airlines and American Eagle operate out of 10 hubs, with Dallas/Fort Worth being its largest; handling more than 200 million passengers annually with an average of more than 500,000 passengers daily. American operates its primary maintenance base in Tulsa in addition to the maintenance locations at its hubs. As of 2019, the company employs nearly 130,000 people.

---

* https://en.wikipedia.org/wiki/American_Airlines

American Airlines, Inc. (AA)는 Texas주 Fort Worth에 본사가 있는 미국의 주요 항공사로서 보유 항공기, 매출액, 승객 수, 취항지로 평가한다면 세계에서 가장 큰 항공사라고 할 수 있다. 1999년 American Airlines는 British Airways, Cathay Pacific, Finnair, Japan Airlines, Malaysia Airlines, Qantas와 함께 항공 동맹인 Oneworld를 설립하였으며, 2017년 현재 승객 수에서 SkyTeam과 Star Alliance에 이어 세 번째로 큰 동맹사이다.

Smart Vocabulary

metroplex: 복합[광역] 대도시권
fleet: (항공기의) 기단(機團); 함대; 선대(船隊)
regional: 지방의; 지역적인
extensive: 광대한, 넓은; 광범위한
found: 설립하다; 세우다
alliance: 동맹; 협력, 제휴
annually: 해마다(yearly), 연 1회
maintenance: 유지; 보수

66. United Airlines *

United Airlines, Inc. is a major American airline headquartered at Willis Tower in Chicago, Illinois. It is the third largest airline in the world, measured by fleet size and route network. United operates a large domestic and international route network, with an extensive presence in the Asia-Pacific region. It is a founding member of the Star Alliance, the world's largest airline alliance with a total of 28 member airlines. Regional service is operated by independent carriers under the brand name United Express. United was established by the amalgamation of several airlines in the late 1920s, the oldest of these being Varney Air Lines, which was founded in 1926.

United has eight hubs, with Chicago–O'Hare being its largest in terms of passengers carried and the number of departures.

* https://en.wikipedia.org/wiki/United_Airlines

United Airlines는 1920년대 후반 Varney Air Lines를 비롯한 여러 항공사들의 합병을 통해 설립되었으며, 가장 큰 허브 공항인 Chicago-O'Hare 공항을 비롯해서 8개의 허브 공항을 갖고 있다. United Airlines는 2010년 Continental Airlines과 합병했으며, American Airlines에 이어 미국 제2위의 항공사로서 Illinois주 Chicago에 본사가 있다. United Airlines는 1997년 5월 14일 설립된 Star Alliance의 창단 회원사이며, Star Alliance에는 Asiana Airlines, Air Canada, Air China, India Air, Air New Zealand, Austrian Airlines, Lufthansa, Thai Airways, Turkish Airlines등이 있으며, 세계에서 가장 큰 항공사 동맹이라고 할 수 있다.

Smart Vocabulary

amalgamation: (회사·사업의) 합병, 합동

67. Delta Air Lines *

Delta Air Lines, Inc., typically referred to as Delta, is one of the major airlines of the United States and a legacy carrier. It is headquartered in Atlanta, Georgia. The airline, along with its subsidiaries and regional affiliates, including Delta Connection, operates over 5,400 flights daily and serves 325 destinations in 52 countries on six continents. Delta is a founding member of the SkyTeam airline alliance.

Delta has nine hubs, with Atlanta being its largest in terms of total passengers and number of departures. It is ranked second among the world's largest airlines by number of scheduled passengers carried, revenue passenger-kilometers flown, and fleet size. It is ranked 69th on the Fortune 500.

---

* https://en.wikipedia.org/wiki/Delta_Air_Lines

Delta Air Lines, Inc.는 1925년 여름 Louisiana 주 Monroe에 설립된 Huff Daland Dusters Inc.에서 농약 살포를 하는 항공사로 출발했으며, 본사는 Georgia 주 Atlanta에 있다. 2008년 10월 당시 미국 항공업계 3위 항공사인 Delta Air Lines은 6위 항공사인 Northwest Airlines(NWA)를 합병하여 세계 최대의 항공사가 되었다. Delta Air Lines는 2000년 6월 22일 설립된 항공 동맹 SkyTeam의 설립 멤버이며, SkyTeam에는 Korean Air를 비롯하여 Aeroflot, Air France, Alitalia, China Airlines, Czech Airlines, Garuda Indonesia, KLM, Vietnam Airlines등 19개 항공사가 속해 있다.

Smart Vocabulary

typically: 전형적(상징적)으로
refer~ to ... as _ : …을 —의 이름으로 부르다
legacy: 유산; 이어(물려)받은 것
affiliate: 계열(자매) 회사
alliance: 동맹

68. Washington D.C. *

Washington D.C., (formally the District of Columbia and commonly referred to as D.C., Washington, or The District) is the capital of the United States. Founded after the American Revolution as the seat of government of the newly independent country, Washington was named after George Washington, the first president of the United States and a Founding Father. As the seat of the United States federal government and several international organizations, Washington is an important world political capital. The city, located on the Potomac River bordering Maryland and Virginia, is one of the most visited cities in the world, with more than 20 million tourists annually.

The signing of the Residence Act on July 16, 1790, approved the creation of a capital district located along the Potomac River on the country's East Coast. The U.S. Constitution provided for a federal district under the exclusive jurisdiction of the U.S. Congress, and the District is therefore not a part of any U.S. state. The states of Maryland and Virginia each donated land to form the federal district, which included the pre-existing settlements of Georgetown and Alexandria. The City of Washington was founded in 1791 to serve as the new national capital. In 1846, Congress returned the land originally ceded by Virginia, including the city of Alexandria; in 1871, it created a single municipal government for the remaining portion of the District.

---

* https://en.wikipedia.org/wiki/Washington,_D.C.

Washington D.C.는 영국과의 전쟁 이후 새롭게 독립한 나라의 중심지로 설립되었으며, 초대 대통령인 George Washington의 이름을 따서 명명되었다. 미국 연방 정부와 몇몇 국제 기구의 중심지로서, Washington D.C.는 중요한 세계 정치 수도이다. 1790년 7월 16일 Residence Act는 동부 해안의 Potomac River를 따라 위치한 수도로서의 지역 건설을 승인했다. 미국 헌법은 의회의 배타적 관할 하에 연방 지역을 규정했으며 그 지역은 미국의 어떤 주에도 속하지 않는다. Maryland 주와 Virginia 주는 각각 연방 지역을 만들기 위해 토지를 기증했는데, 그 지역은 Georgetown과 Alexandria가 포함되어 있었다. The City of Washington는 1791년에 새로운 국가의 수도로서 설립되었고, 1846년 의회는 Alexandria를 포함하여 Virginia가 양도한 땅을 반환하였고, 1871년에 그 지역의 나머지 지역에 단일 자치 정부를 설립하였다.

Smart Vocabulary

American Revolution: 미국의 독립 혁명, 독립 전쟁
seat: (활동의) 소재지, 중심지
Founding Father: (1789년의) 합중국 헌법 제정자들
federal government: 《美》 연방 정부
border: 접경하다, 접하다
residence: 주거, 주택
Act: (종종 A-) 법령, 조례
Constitution: 헌법
exclusive: 배타적(제외적)인
jurisdiction: 재판권, 사법권
settlement: 정착, 정주(定住); 정주지
cede: 인도(引渡)하다, (권리를) 양도하다
municipal; 시(市)의, 도시의, 자치 도시의

69. New York City *

New York City (NYC), also known as the City of New York or simply New York (NY), is the most populous city in the United States. With an estimated 2018 population of 8,398,748 distributed over about 302.6 square miles (784 km2), New York is also the most densely populated major city in the United States. Located at the southern tip of the U.S. state of New York, the city is the center of the New York metropolitan area, the largest metropolitan area in the world by urban landmass and one of the world's most populous megacities. New York City has been described as the cultural capital of the world, and exerts a significant impact upon commerce, entertainment, research, technology, education, politics, tourism, art, fashion, and sports. Home to the headquarters of the United Nations, New York is an important center for international diplomacy.

Situated on one of the world's largest natural harbors, New York City is divided into five administrative boroughs, each of which is a separate county of the State of New York. The five boroughs – Brooklyn, Queens, Manhattan, The Bronx, and Staten Island – were consolidated into a single city in 1898. The city and its metropolitan area constitute the premier gateway for legal immigration to the United States. As many as 800 languages are spoken in New York, making it the most linguistically diverse city in the world. New York is home to 3.2 million residents born outside the United States, the largest foreign-born population of any city in the world as of 2016. As of 2019, the New York metropolitan area is estimated to produce a gross metropolitan product (GMP) of US$2.0 trillion. If greater New York City were a sovereign state, it would have the 12th highest GDP in the world. It is home to the highest number of billionaires of any city in the world.

---

* https://en.wikipedia.org/wiki/New_York_City

New York은 미국에서 가장 인구가 많고 인구 밀도가 높은 도시로서 세계의 문화 수도로 불린다. New York은 Brooklyn, Queens, Manhattan, The Bronx, Staten Island 다섯 개의 독립된 자치구로 나뉘어 있으며, 1898년 New York City로 합병되었다. New York은 1624년 Dutch Republic의 식민지 개척자들이 Lower Manhattan에 교역소를 설립하였고, 1626년 New Amsterdam이라고 불렸다. 1664년 이곳은 영국인들의 통치아래 있었고, King Charles II가 동생 Duke of York에게 그 땅을 준 이후 New York이라고 불리기 시작하였다.

Smart Vocabulary

distribute: 분포시키다, (골고루) 퍼뜨리다
landmass: 광대한 토지; 대륙
exert: 발휘하다; (영향력·압력 등을) 행사하다
consolidate: 합병하다, 통합하다
borough: 자치 읍면 《어떤 주의》; (New York시의) 독립구
premier: 첫째의; 최초의
immigration: 이주, 이입, 입국
linguistically: 어학(상)적으로
gross: 총체의, 전반적인, 총계의(total)
sovereign: 독립한, 자주적인

New York City traces its origins to a trading post founded by colonists from the Dutch Republic in 1624 on Lower Manhattan; the post was named New Amsterdam in 1626. The city and its surroundings came under English control in 1664 and were renamed New York after King Charles II of England granted the lands to his brother, the Duke of York. New York was the capital of the United States from 1785 until 1790, and has been the largest US city since 1790. The Statue of Liberty greeted millions of immigrants as they came to the U.S. by ship in the late 19th and early 20th centuries and is an international symbol of the U.S. and its ideals of liberty and peace. In the 21st century, New York has emerged as a global node of creativity and entrepreneurship, social tolerance, and environmental sustainability, and as a symbol of freedom and cultural diversity. In 2019, New York was voted the greatest city in the world per a survey of over 30,000 people from 48 cities worldwide, citing its cultural diversity.

Smart Vocabulary

trading post: 교역소
colonist: 식민지 개척자
Dutch: (the ~) 네덜란드 사람
immigrant: 이주자, 이민
emerge: 나타나다
node: 중심점
entrepreneurship: 기업가 정신
tolerance: 관용; 아량, 포용력
sustainability: 지속 가능성
diversity: 다양성; 차이(점); 변화(variety)

70. Boston *

Boston is the capital and most populous city of the Commonwealth of Massachusetts in the United States, and the 21st most populous city in the United States. The city proper covers 49 square miles (127 km2) with an estimated population of 694,583 in 2018, also making it the most populous city in New England. Boston is the seat of Suffolk County as well, although the county government was disbanded on July 1, 1999. The city is the economic and cultural anchor of a substantially larger metropolitan area known as Greater Boston, a metropolitan statistical area (MSA) home to a census-estimated 4.8 million people in 2016 and ranking as the tenth-largest such area in the country. As a combined statistical area (CSA), this wider commuting region is home to some 8.2 million people, making it the sixth most populous in the United States.

Boston is one of the oldest municipalities in the United States, founded on the Shawmut Peninsula in 1630 by Puritan settlers from the English town of the same name. It was the scene of several key events of the American Revolution, such as the Boston Massacre, the Boston Tea Party, the Battle of Bunker Hill, and the Siege of Boston. Upon gaining U.S. independence from Great Britain, it continued to be an important port and manufacturing hub as well as a center for education and culture. The city has expanded beyond the original peninsula through land reclamation and municipal annexation. Its rich history attracts many tourists, with Faneuil Hall alone drawing more than 20 million visitors per year. Boston's many firsts include the United States' first public park (Boston Common, 1634), first public or state school (Boston Latin School, 1635)[18] and first subway system (Tremont Street Subway, 1897).

---

* https://en.wikipedia.org/wiki/Boston

Boston은 Massachusetts의 주도이자 가장 인구가 많은 도시이며, 미국에서 21번째로 인구가 많은 도시이다. Boston은 1630년 똑같은 이름의 영국 도시에서 온 청교도 이주민들에 의해 Shawmut Peninsula에 세운 가장 오래된 도시 중 하나이다. Boston Massacre, the Boston Tea Party, the Battle of Bunker Hill, the Siege of Boston과 같은 미국의 독립전쟁의 주요 사건들이 일어난 곳이다. 미국이 영국으로부터 독립한 후에도 Boston은 그곳은 교육과 문화의 중심지뿐만 아니라 중요한 항구이자 제조업의 중심지였다.

Smart Vocabulary

the Commonwealth: 《美》주
proper: (흔히 명사 뒤에 와서) 본래의, 진정한; 엄격한 의미로서의
disband: 해산하다
substantially: 대체로; 사실상
commute: 통근(통학)하다
American Revolution: 미국의 독립 혁명, 독립 전쟁
reclamation: 개발, 간척, 개간
municipal: 시(市)의, 도시의
annexation: 합병

71. Los Angeles *

Los Angeles (Spanish for "The Angels") is the most populous city in California; the second most populous city in the United States, after New York City; and the third most populous city in North America, after Mexico City and New York City. With an estimated population of nearly four million people, Los Angeles is the cultural, financial, and commercial center of Southern California. The city is known for its Mediterranean climate, ethnic diversity, Hollywood, the entertainment industry, and its sprawling metropolis.

Los Angeles lies in a basin in Southern California, adjacent to the Pacific Ocean, with mountains as high as 10,000 feet (3,000 m), and deserts. The city, which covers about 469 square miles (1,210 km2), is the seat of Los Angeles County, the most populous county in the United States. The Los Angeles metropolitan area (MSA) is the second-largest metropolitan area in the nation with a population of 13.1 million people. Greater Los Angeles, which includes the metro area of Riverside and San Bernardino, is the nation's second most populous combined statistical area, with a 2015 estimate of 18.7 million people.

Historically home to the Chumash and Tongva, Los Angeles was claimed by Juan Rodríguez Cabrillo for Spain in 1542. The city was officially founded on September 4, 1781, by Spanish governor Felipe de Neve. It became a part of Mexico in 1821 following the Mexican War of Independence. In 1848, at the end of the Mexican–American War, Los Angeles and the rest of California were purchased as part of the Treaty of Guadalupe Hidalgo, and thus became part of the United States. Los Angeles was incorporated as a municipality on April 4, 1850, five months before California achieved statehood. The discovery of oil in the 1890s brought rapid growth to the city. The city was further expanded with the completion of the Los Angeles Aqueduct in 1913, which delivers water from Eastern California.

---

* https://en.wikipedia.org/wiki/Los_Angeles

Los Angeles (스페인어로 "천사들")는 California주에서 가장 인구가 많은 도시이며, New York City에 이어 두 번째로 인구가 많은 도시이다. Los Angeles는 Southern California의 문화, 금융, 상업 중심지이며, 지중해의 기후, 인종적 다양성, Hollywood, 엔터테인먼트 산업, 그리고 대도시로 알려져 있다. Los Angeles는 1781년 9월 4일 스페인의 통치자 Felipe de Neve가 공식적으로 세웠으며, 1821년 멕시코 독립 전쟁으로 인해 멕시코의 일부가 된다. 1848년 멕시코-미국의 전쟁이 끝날 무렵, Los Angeles와 California의 나머지 지역은 Treaty of Guadalupe Hidalgo의 일환으로 매입되어 미국의 일부가 되었다.

Smart Vocabulary

Mediterranean: 지중해(의)
ethnic: 인종의, 민족의
diversity: 다양성; 차이(점)
sprawl: 손발을 쭉 뻗다; (불규칙하게) 퍼지다
metropolis: 수도(capital); 중심도시
basin: 분지
adjacent: 접근한, 인접한, 부근의
statistical: 통계(상)의; 통계학의
estimate: 평가, 견적
statehood: 국가(주)로서의 지위
municipality: 자치제
aqueduct: 도수관(導水管), 수도

72. Las Vegas *

Las Vegas (Spanish for "The Meadows"), officially the City of Las Vegas and often known simply as Vegas, is the 28th-most populated city in the United States, the most populated city in the state of Nevada, and the county seat of Clark County. The city anchors the Las Vegas Valley metropolitan area and is the largest city within the greater Mojave Desert. Las Vegas is an internationally renowned major resort city, known primarily for its gambling, shopping, fine dining, entertainment, and nightlife. The Las Vegas Valley as a whole serves as the leading financial, commercial, and cultural center for Nevada.

The city bills itself as The Entertainment Capital of the World, and is famous for its mega casino–hotels and associated activities. It is a top three destination in the United States for business conventions and a global leader in the hospitality industry, claiming more AAA Five Diamond hotels than any other city in the world. Today, Las Vegas annually ranks as one of the world's most visited tourist destinations. The city's tolerance for numerous forms of adult entertainment earned it the title of "Sin City", and has made Las Vegas a popular setting for literature, films, television programs, and music videos.

Las Vegas was settled in 1905 and officially incorporated in 1911. At the close of the 20th century, it was the most populated American city founded within that century (a similar distinction was earned by Chicago in the 19th century). Population growth has accelerated since the 1960s, and between 1990 and 2000 the population nearly doubled, increasing by 85.2%. Rapid growth has continued into the 21st century, and according to estimates from the U.S. Census Bureau, the city had 648,224 residents in 2018, with a metropolitan population of 2,227,053.

---

* https://en.wikipedia.org/wiki/Las_Vegas

Las Vegas (스페인어로 "초원")는 미국에서 28번째로 인구가 가장 많은 도시이며, Nevada 주에서 인구가 가장 많은 도시다. Las Vegas는 주로 도박, 쇼핑, 근사한 식사, 유흥, 그리고 밤 문화로 유명한 휴양 도시이며, 전체적으로 Nevada 주의 선도적인 금융, 상업 및 문화의 중심지로서의 역할을 한다. Las Vegas는 거대한 카지노-호텔과 관련된 활동들로 유명해서 스스로 "The Entertainment Capital of the World"라고 광고하고 있으며, 수많은 형태의 성인 오락물에 대한 관용은 "Sin City"라는 이름을 얻게 했고, 이는 이 도시를 문학, 영화, 텔레비전 프로그램, 뮤직 비디오의 인기 있는 배경으로 만들었다.

Smart Vocabulary

seat: (활동의) 소재지, 중심지
renowned: 유명한, 명성이 있는
as a whole: 전체로서, 총괄하여
bill: 전단으로 광고(발표)하다
associated: 관련된
hospitality: 환대, 후한 대접
tolerance: 관용
incorporate: 통합(합병, 편입)하다
distinction: 구별, 차별; 특성, 특질

73. Alaska *

Alaska is a state located in the northwest extremity of the North American West Coast, just across the Bering Strait from Asia. An exclave of the U.S., it borders the Canadian province of British Columbia and territory of Yukon to the east and southeast has a maritime border with Russia's Chukotka Autonomous Okrug to the west. To the north are the Chukchi and Beaufort seas of the Arctic Ocean, while the Pacific Ocean lies to the south and southwest.

Alaska is the largest U.S. state by area and the seventh largest subnational division in the world. It is the third least populous and the most sparsely populated state, but by far the continent's most populous territory located mostly north of the 60th parallel, with an estimated population of 738,432 as 2015 — more than quadruple the combined populations of Northern Canada and Greenland. Approximately half of Alaska's residents live within the Anchorage metropolitan area. The state capital of Juneau is the second largest city in the United States by area, comprising more territory than the states of Rhode Island and Delaware.

Alaska was occupied by various indigenous peoples for thousands of years before the arrival of Europeans. The state is considered the entry point for the settlement of North America by way of the Bering land bridge. The Russians were the first non-native people to settle the area beginning in the 18th century, eventually establishing the colony of Alaska that spanned most of the current state. The expense and difficulty of maintaining this distant possession prompted its sale to the U.S. in 1867 for $7.2 million, or approximately two cents per acre ($4.74/km2). The area went through several administrative changes before becoming organized as a territory on May 11, 1912. It was admitted as the 49th state of the U.S. on January 3, 1959.

---

* https://en.wikipedia.org/wiki/Alaska

Alaska는 면적으로는 미국에서 가장 큰 주이고 인구는 세 번째로 적지만, 위도 60도 선의 가장 북쪽에 위치한 대륙에서 가장 인구가 많은 지역이다. Alaska는 유럽인들의 도착 이전 수천 년 동안 다양한 토착민들이 점령했고, 러시아인들은 18세기 초부터 이 지역에 정착한 최초의 비원주민들이었으며 결국 현재의 대부분의 주에 걸쳐 있는 Alaska 식민지를 건설했다. 러시아는 멀리 떨어진 땅을 유지하는 비용과 어려움으로 인해 1867년 미국에 에이커 당 약 2센트에 팔았다. Alaska는 1912년 5월 11일 하나의 영토가 되기 전에 몇 번의 행정적 변화를 겪었고, 1959년 1월 3일 미국의 49번째 주가 된다.

Smart Vocabulary

extremity: 끝, 말단
strait: 해협
exclave: 본국에서 떨어져 다른 나라 영토에 둘러싸인 영토
maritime: 바다의; 해변의, 해안의
the Arctic Ocean: 북극해
sparsely: 희박하게
parallel: 위도권(圈), 위도선
quadruple: 4배의
metropolitan: 수도(권)의; 대도시의
comprise: 포함하다; …으로 이루어져 있다; 구성하다
land bridge: 〖地〗 육교(陸橋) 《육지와 육지, 또는 육지와 섬을 잇는 띠 모양의 육지》

74. Hawaii *

Hawaiʻi is a state of the United States of America. It is the only state located in the Pacific Ocean and the only state composed entirely of islands.

The state encompasses nearly the entire Hawaiian archipelago, 137 islands spread over 1,500 miles (2,400 km). The volcanic archipelago is physiographically and ethnologically part of the Polynesian subregion of Oceania. At the southeastern end of the archipelago, the eight main islands are, in order from northwest to southeast: Niʻihau, Kauaʻi, Oʻahu, Molokaʻi, Lānaʻi, Kahoʻolawe, Maui, and Hawaiʻi. The last is the largest island in the group; it is often called the "Big Island" or "Hawaiʻi Island" to avoid confusion with the state or archipelago.

Hawaiʻi is the 8th-smallest geographically and the 11th-least populous, but the 13th-most densely populated of the 50 states. It is the only state with an Asian American plurality. Hawaii has more than 1.4 million permanent residents, along with many visitors and U.S. military personnel. The state capital and largest city is Honolulu on the island of Oʻahu. The state's ocean coastline is about 750 miles (1,210 km) long, the fourth longest in the U.S., after the coastlines of Alaska, Florida, and California. Hawaii is the most recent state to join the union, on August 21, 1959. It was an independent nation until 1898.

---

* https://en.wikipedia.org/wiki/Hawaii

> Hawaii는 모든 Hawaii의 군도 전체를 포함하고 있으며, 137개 섬이 2,400km에 걸쳐 퍼져 있고 특히 Niʻihau, Kauaʻi, Oʻahu, Molokaʻi, Lānaʻi, Kahoʻolawe, Maui, Hawaiʻi 8개의 주요 섬이 있다. 이 중에서 Oʻahu섬에 Waikiki 해변이 있으며, 가장 큰 섬인 Hawaiʻi는 "Big Island"나 "Hawaiʻi Island"라고 불린다.

Smart Vocabulary

encompass: 포함하다; 둘러(에워)싸다
archipelago: 군도(群島); 섬 많은 바다
volcanic: 화산의; 화산성의
physiographically: 지형학적으로
ethnologically: 민족[인종]학적으로
subregion: 소구역(小區域), 소지역
confusion: 혼동, 혼란
geographically: 지리(학)적으로
plurality: 다수, 대다수, 과반수
personnel: 전직원, 인원
capital: 수도; 중심지

Heritage Sites of Hawaii *

Bishop Museum

Founded in 1889, the Bernice Pauahi Bishop Museum is the premier natural and cultural history institution in the Pacific region, housing more than 24 million cultural and natural treasures from Hawaii and Polynesia.

Leahi (Diamond Head) State Monument

The iconic crater sitting at the edge of Waikiki is named Leahi (forehead of the ahi fish) due to its profile resembling that of the fish. Visitors can hike a trail to the summit to see stunning views of the south shore of the island.

Iolani Palace State Monument

Built in 1882 by King Kalakaua, Iolani Palace was home to Hawaii's last reigning monarchs and is registered as a National Historic Landmark. The public is welcome to visit on guided tours.

National Memorial Cemetery of the Pacific

The history of the United States military in Hawaii reaches back to the late 1800s. Also called "Punchbowl" for its location inside a crater, the National Memorial Cemetery of the Pacific was established in 1949 as a final resting place for those who served in the armed forces.

---

* https://www.gohawaii.com/experiences/history-culture

Bishop Museum은 1889년 Charles Reed Bishop이 설립했으며, King Kamehameha I 왕족의 유물을 포함하여 전 세계에서 Polynesian 문화 유물을 가장 많이 수집하고 있고 가장 유명한 박물관이다. Diamond Head는 Waikiki 해변의 동쪽에 있는 분화구로서 동굴과 계단을 통과해서 정상에 오르면 Waikiki와 Honolulu 전경을 한눈에 볼 수 있다. Iolani Palace는 Kalakaua왕이 1882년에 건설한 궁전으로 Kamehameha 왕조에서 통치자들의 거처였고 1978년부터 박물관으로 사용된다. National Memorial Cemetery of the Pacific는 제1·2차 세계대전에서부터 베트남 전쟁까지 미군에 복무했던 사람들을 위한 공동묘지로서 1949년에 건설되었으며, 분화구 안에 위치해서 Punchbowl이라고 불린다.

Smart Vocabulary

premier: 첫째의; 최초의
institution: (공공) 시설, (공공) 기관, 학회, 협회
crater: 분화구
ahi: 하와이의 큰눈 참치
profile: 옆모습, 측면; 윤곽
stunning: 기절할 만큼의; 《口》 근사한, 멋진
monument: 기념비, 기념 건조물, 기념탑
reign: 군림하다, 지배
monarch: 군주, 제왕
memorial: 기념의; 추도의
cemetery: 묘지
punchbowl: 펀치 담는 그릇; (산간(山間)의) 주발같이 우묵한 곳, 분지(盆地)
resting place: 휴식처; 무덤
armed forces: (육·해·공의) 군, 군대; 전군

Nuuanu Pali State Wayside

The lookout on these steep cliffs offer panoramic views of the Koolau mountain range and the east side of the island. This was the site of the Battle of Nuuanu, where Kamehameha the Great defeated Oahu forces and brought the island under his rule.

Pearl Harbor

On Dec. 7, 1941, Oahu was struck by a surprise Japanese military attack that pulled America into World War II. Most of the destruction was centered at Pearl Harbor. Today, visitors can learn about that pivotal point in world history at the Pearl Harbor National Memorial, which includes the USS Arizona Memorial.

Waikiki*

Located on the south shore of Honolulu, the world-famous neighborhood of Waikiki was once a playground for Hawaiian royalty. Known in Hawaiian as "spouting waters," Waikiki was introduced to the world when its first hotel, the Moana Surfrider, was built on its shores in 1901. Today, Waikiki is Oahu's main hotel and resort area and a vibrant gathering place for visitors from around the world. Along the main strip of Kalakaua Avenue you'll find world-class shopping, dining, entertainment, activities and resorts.

---

* https://www.gohawaii.com/islands/oahu/regions/honolulu/Waikiki

Nuuanu Pali State Wayside는 Nu□uanu Valley의 위쪽 가파른 절벽에 위치한 전망대이다.

Pearl Harbor는 1941년 12월 7일, 일본이 기습적으로 Oahu를 공습하였고 대부분의 파괴가 집중된 곳이다. 이 날은 "date which will live in infamy"로 전 세계에 알려졌으며, 이로 인해 미국이 2차 세계 대전에 참전하게 된다. Waikiki는 Honolulu의 남쪽 해안에 위치한 해변 휴양지로서 과거 Hawaii 왕족들의 놀이터였으며, Hawaii어로 "내뿜는 물"이라는 뜻을 갖고 있다.

Smart Vocabulary

wayside: 길가(의), 노변(의)
lookout: 조망, 전망
steep: 가파른, 깎아지른 듯한
range: 산맥; 목장
defeat: 쳐부수다
pivotal: 중추의, 중요한
royalty: 왕권, 왕위; (보통 pl.) 왕족
spout: 내뿜다; 분출하다
vibrant: 활력이 넘치는; (사람이) 활발한
strip: 좁고 긴 땅

Duke Kahanamoku *

On Kuhio Beach, a bronze statue of Duke Kahanamoku welcomes you to Waikiki with open arms. Duke was a true Hawaiian hero and one of the world's greatest watermen, a master of swimming, surfing and outrigger canoe paddling.

Aloha Tower **

Located on the Honolulu Harbor in Downtown Honolulu, about 15 minutes west of Waikiki, Aloha Tower is an iconic symbol of Hawaii. Built in September of 1926, this was the tallest building in the islands for four decades and its clock was one of the largest in the United States. The tower stood as a welcoming beacon for visitors since travel to Oahu was done entirely by sea. Duke Kahanamoku set his first swimming world record here at Pier 7 and the wharf was also known for Boat Days, a lively celebration to welcome the arrival of visiting ships.

Statue of King Kamehameha I ***

A great warrior, diplomat and leader, King Kamehameha I united the Hawaiian Islands into one royal kingdom in 1810 after years of conflict. You can still visit the Nuuanu Pali Lookout, the site of the Battle of Nuuanu, a crucial conflict that helped Kamehameha conquer Oahu.

---

* https://www.gohawaii.com/islands/oahu/regions/honolulu/duke-kahanamoku-statue
** https://www.gohawaii.com/islands/oahu/regions/honolulu/aloha-tower
*** https://www.gohawaii.com/islands/oahu/regions/honolulu/king-kamehameha-statue

Duke Kahanamoku는 Waikiki의 Kuhio Beach에서 볼 수 있는 청동 동상으로서, Hawaii의 진정한 영웅이며 "The father of modern surfing"로 인정받는다. Aloha Tower는 Waikiki에서 서쪽으로 15분 거리에 있는 Honolulu Harbor에 위치하고 있으며, 1926년 9월에 지어진 이후 Oahu를 방문하는 사람들을 환영하는 등대와 같은 역할을 했다. King Kamehameha I 는 위대한 전사, 외교관, 지도자로서 1810년 수 년 간의 싸움 끝에 Hawaii 섬들을 하나의 왕국으로 통합했다.

Smart Vocabulary

statue: 상(像), 조상(彫像)
outrigger: 〖海〗현외(舷外)장치; 현외로 내민 노걸이 받침쇠(가 있는 보트)
paddle: 노를 젓다
beacon: 등대; 신호소; 〔항공, 교통〕표지
pier: 부두; 방파제
wharf: 부두, 선창(pier)
conflict: 싸움; 대립; 〖心〗갈등
crucial: 결정적인, 중대한

Dole Plantation *

Journey through the 2008 World's Largest Maze, as featured in the Guinness Book of World Records, where fearless adventurers can search for eight secret stations on their way to solving the mystery of the maze. Then, take a ride on the Pineapple Express train. This 20-minute train tour is fully narrated in English, Japanese, Korean and Mandarin, and will give visitors an overview on the history of the pineapple, agriculture in Hawaii, and the life of James Dole. Trains depart every half-hour between 9:30 am and 5:00 pm, weather permitting. Next, stroll through the Plantation Garden Tour. The tour consists of eight mini-gardens that will give visitors a close-up look at a wide variety of fruits, flowers and native plants. Tour-goers will hear stories and legends of old Hawaii. The audio narration is available in English, Japanese and Korean.

Polynesian Cultural Center **

The Polynesian Cultural Center is Hawaii's #1 visitor attraction, has 6 island villages representing the unique island cultures of Hawaii, Fiji, Aotearoa (New Zealand), Samoa, Tahiti, and Tonga.

Set on 42 acres along Oahu's North Shore, the Polynesian Cultural Center has a lagoon that hosts daily canoe tours and an exciting cultural Canoe Pageant.

Our award-winning Ali'i Luau takes guests on a journey to learn about Hawaii's royalty while enjoying traditional Polynesian food and entertainment.

You can also enjoy our immersive cinema presentation "Hawaiian Journey", a tribute to the splendors of Hawaii.

---

* https://www.gohawaii.com/listing/dole-plantation/494
** https://www.gohawaii.com/listing/polynesian-cultural-center/708

Dole Plantation은 2008년 세계에서 가장 큰 미로를 여행하는 곳으로 20분 동안 Pineapple Express 열차를 타고 파인애플의 역사, Hawaii의 농업, James Dole의 삶에 대해 알게 된다. 그리고 Plantation Garden Tour는 8개의 미니 정원을 돌아보며 Hawaii의 옛 이야기와 전설을 듣게 된다. Polynesian Cultural Center는 Hawaii 최고의 관광 명소로서 Hawaii, Fiji, Aotearoa (New Zealand), Samoa, Tahiti, Tonga의 독특한 섬 문화를 보여주는 6개의 섬 마을로 이루어져 있다.

Smart Vocabulary

overview: 개관, 개략
weather permitting: 날씨만 좋으면
stroll: 산책하다
represent: 묘사하다; 말로 표현하다; 대표하다
lagoon: 개펄, 석호(潟湖)
pageant: 야외극, 구경거리
immersive: 몰입형(沒入型)의
tribute: 찬사, 칭찬

75. Guam *

Guam is an organized territory of the United States in Micronesia in the western Pacific Ocean. It is the westernmost point and territory of the United States, along with the Northern Mariana Islands. The capital city of Guam is Hagåtña and the most populous city is Dededo. Guam has been a member of the Pacific Community since 1983. The inhabitants of Guam are called Guamanians, and they are American citizens by birth. The indigenous Guamanians are the Chamorros, who are related to other Austronesian natives of Eastern Indonesia, the Philippines, and Taiwan.

The indigenous Chamorros settled the island approximately 4,000 years ago. Portuguese explorer Ferdinand Magellan, while in the service of Spain, was the first European to visit the island, on March 6, 1521. Guam was colonized by Spain in 1668 with settlers, including Diego Luis de San Vitores, a Catholic Jesuit missionary. Between the 16th century and the 18th century, Guam was an important stopover for the Spanish Manila Galleons. During the Spanish–American War, the United States captured Guam on June 21, 1898. Under the Treaty of Paris, Spain ceded Guam to the United States on December 10, 1898. Guam is among the 17 non-self-governing territories listed by the United Nations.

Before World War II, there were five American jurisdictions in the Pacific Ocean: Guam and Wake Island in Micronesia, American Samoa and Hawaii in Polynesia, and the Philippines.

On December 8, 1941, hours after the attack on Pearl Harbor, Guam was captured by the Japanese, who occupied the island for two and a half years. During the occupation, Guamanians were subjected to beheadings, forced labor, rape, and torture. American forces recaptured the island on July 21, 1944; Liberation Day commemorates the victory.

---

* https://en.wikipedia.org/wiki/Guam

Guam은 Micronesia에 있는 미국의 자치령으로서 Northern Mariana Islands와 함께 미국의 가장 서쪽 지역의 영토이다. 토착민 Chamorro들은 약 4,000년 전에 섬에 정착했으며, 포르투갈의 탐험가인 Ferdinand Magellan은 1521년 3월 6일 Guam을 방문한 첫 번째 유럽인이었다. Guam은 1668년 스페인에 의해 식민지화되었고, 스페인과 미국의 전쟁으로 인해 미국이 1898년 6월 21일 Guam을 점령했고, 1898년 12월 10일 Treaty of Paris에 따라 스페인은 미국에 Guam을 양도했다. 1941년 12월 8일 Pearl Harbor에 대한 공격이 있은 지 몇 시간 후, Guam은 2년 반 동안 일본인들에 의해 점령당했고, 1944년 7월 21일 미군이 Guam을 탈환했다.

Smart Vocabulary

westernmost: 가장 서쪽의
territory: 영토 ; (본토에서 떨어져 있는) 속령, 보호(자치)령
inhabitant: 주민, 거주자
indigenous: 토착의(native), 그 고장에 고유한; 타고난
approximately: 대략, 대강
Jesuit: 〖가톨릭〗제수이트 수사《the Society of Jesus의 수사》
missionary: 선교사
stopover: 단기 체재(지)
capture: 점령(공략)하다
treaty: 조약, 협정
cede: 인도(引渡)하다, (권리를) 양도하다
jurisdiction: 관할권; 재판권, 사법권
behead: 목을 베다, 참수하다
be subjected to: …을 받다[당하다]
commemorate: (…을) 기념하다, 축하하다

76. Saipan *

Saipan is the largest island of the Northern Mariana Islands, a commonwealth of the United States in the western Pacific Ocean. According to 2017 estimates by the United States Census Bureau, Saipan's population was 52,263.

The legislative and executive branches of Commonwealth government are located in the village of Capitol Hill on the island; the judicial branch is headquartered in the village of Susupe. Since the entire island is organized as a single municipality, most publications designate Saipan as the Commonwealth's capital.

As of June 12, 2015 the Mayor of Saipan is David M. Apatang.

World War II

Japan considered Saipan to be part of the last line of defenses for the Japanese homeland, and thus had strongly committed to defending it. The Imperial Japanese Army and Imperial Japanese Navy garrisoned Saipan heavily from the late 1930s, building numerous coastal artillery batteries, shore defenses, underground fortifications and an airstrip. In mid-1944, nearly 30,000 troops were based on the island.

The Battle of Saipan from 15 June to 9 July 1944 was one of the major campaigns of World War II. The United States Marine Corps and United States Army landed on the beaches of the southwestern side of the island, and spent more than three weeks in heavy fighting to secure the island from the Japanese. The battle cost the Americans 3,426 killed and 10,364 wounded, whereas of the estimated 30,000 Japanese defenders, only 921 were taken prisoner. Weapons and the tactics of close quarter fighting also resulted in high civilian casualties. Some 20,000 Japanese civilians perished during the battle, including over 1,000 who committed suicide by jumping from "Suicide Cliff" and "Banzai Cliff" rather than be taken prisoner.

---

* https://en.wikipedia.org/wiki/Saipan

Saipan은 미국의 연방인 Northern Mariana Islands중에서 가장 큰 섬이며, 2017년 미국 인구 조사국의 추정에 따르면, 인구는 52,263명이다. 1521년 스페인 Ferdinand Magellan의 탐험대가 이 섬을 발견했고, 1668년 공식적으로 이 섬을 점령하여 San José라고 불렀다. 1898년 스페인과 미국의 전쟁 이후 미국이 Saipan을 점령했지만, 1899년 스페인에 의해 독일 제국에 팔렸고 German New Guinea의 일부로 독일에 의해 관리되었다. 1914년 제1차 세계 대전 동안, 일본이 Saipan을 점령했고 1919년 League of Nations에 의해 공식적인 통제권을 부여 받았다. 제2차 세계 대전 후 Saipan은 미국이 관리하는 Trust Territory of the Pacific Islands의 일부가 되었고, 1978년 이래 Northern Mariana Islands의 연방 자치령이 되었다.

Smart Vocabulary

the Commonwealth: 《美》주
legislative: 입법(상)의; 입법부의
executive: 행정(상)의; 행정부에 속하는
judicial: 사법의, 재판상의
municipality: 지방 자치제
designate: 가리키다; 지명하다
garrison: 수비하다; (부대를) 주둔시키다
artillery: 포, 대포
battery: 포병 중대; 포대
fortification: 요새화(化); (보통 pl.) 방어 공사, 요새
airstrip: (임시) 활주로; 소(小)공항
troop: (보통 pl.) 군대, 병력
secure: 확보(획득)하다, 얻다, 손에 넣다
tactics: [단수취급] 용병학, 전술(학); [복수취급] (전술의 응용으로서의) 작전
casualty: 사상자, 희생자, 부상자; (pl.) 사상자 수

미국의 사회와 문화

펴낸날 초판 1쇄 발행/ 2020년 2월 28일

지은이 이종문
펴낸이 원병철
편 집 원혜임
펴낸곳 장원문화인쇄
주 소 인천 미추홀구 숭의동 346-3번지
전 화 032-881-4944, 032-428-0070
팩 스 032-881-3237

정가 : 12,000원
ISBN 979-11-960973-5-6